REPORTING R

ANALYSING THE MEDIA
AND THE MONARCHY

EDITED BY JOHN MAIR
AND
ANDREW BECK
WITH
RICHARD LANCE KEEBLE

Copyright © Mair Golden Moments 2023
Published by Mair Golden Moments 2023
Mair Golden Moments asserts
the moral right to be identified as
the author of this work.
Extracts of copyrighted material
used strictly in accordance with
Fair Use commentary provisions.
All copyrights and
trademarks acknowledged.
All rights reserved.
No part of this publication
may be reproduced, stored in
a retrieval system or transmitted
in any form or by any means,
electronic, mechanical, photocopying,
recording, or otherwise,
without prior permission.
While every precaution has been
taken in the preparation of this book,
the publisher assumes no responsibility
for errors or omissions, or for damages
resulting from the use of the
information contained herein.

What the front cover means

Dean Stockton, cover designer

The House of Windsor is at a watershed moment. With the passing of the Queen of Hearts, Queen Elizabeth II, its foundations are now in a precarious state. Akin to a House of Cards, the whole façade is liable to topple at any moment, its stability upheld at the whim of the mass media.

The face of each playing card depicts a member of the current British royal family, as perceived by the public and influenced by the media. The backs of the deck of cards are embellished with the Royal Standard. If one looks closely, the Jacks are replaced with P for Prince and Princess.

King Charles, the King of Diamonds, sits at the top of the edifice supported by Queen Camilla, the Queen of Diamonds. The King and Queen of Diamonds in playing card symbolism generally represents material wealth and treasures; specifically, someone who has inherited a great deal of money or other valuable possessions.

Directly below the King and Queen are William and Kate, represented by the Prince and Princess of Hearts, both adored by the public and media alike.

The next tier features the royal pariahs. Prince Andrew is represented by the Prince of Clubs. Clubs, sometimes known as trefoils, symbolise autumn and the onset of winter, night, darkness, and masculinity. Next to Prince Andrew are Harry and Meghan, represented by the Prince and Princess of Spades. This suit represents bad fortune, disaster, hatred, and even the end of the world . . .

In the shadows at the base of the structure are the minor and former royals, including Prince Edward, the Prince of Diamonds and Princess Anne, the Princess of Diamonds.

The shadowy elements of the media lurk in the background.

Acknowledgements

These hackademic books are labours of love, for the editors and, we hope, for the authors too. They are produced in record time and nobody is paid. I thank them for their insights and patience in the light of heavy nudging.

The biggest thanks for this book goes to my long-time collaborator Professor Richard Lance Keeble. It was his idea but he did not have time to realise it. The end product may also not be as republican as he might have hoped. We are eternally grateful to him.

Other long-term collaborators also worked wonders. Dean Stockton, the genius graphic designer/cover artist, added magic, as did Roger Packer the super sub of Guildford. He made it publishable.

Most of all huge kudos to my friend (still) Andrew Beck who has been the engine room that has kept this liner afloat through some heavy seas.

Our partners, Susan and Helen, deserve praise for their patience.

I hope you enjoy our offering.

John Mair Oxford, England, May 2023

The editors

John Mair was born in the then-British Guiana (to an 'Old Guianese' mother: heritage not age) in 1950. He went to Sacred Heart RC School, in Georgetown. John won the top scholarship in the Common Entrance examination in Guiana in 1961. Then his parents emigrated to the UK. He returns regularly to Guyana. He writes there under the nom de guerre Bill Cotton/Reform. John is the proud owner of a Guyana UK High Commission Award. He attended the LSE, Sussex, and Leeds universities. John has taught journalism at the universities of Coventry, Kent, Northampton, Brunel, Edinburgh Napier, and Guyana and at the Communication University of China. He has edited more than fifty hackademic volumes over the last twelve years on subjects ranging from trust in television, the health of investigative journalism, reporting the Arab Spring, to three volumes on the Leveson Inquiry. His most recent books have been on Inspector Morse in Oxford, ten Oxford authors, reporting the war in Ukraine, and Boris Johnson's time as UK Prime Minister. He created the Coventry Conversations which attracted 350 media movers and shakers to Coventry University. Most recently, he began the My Jericho (Myjericho.co.uk) series of talks in Oxford. In a previous life, he was an award-winning producer/director for the BBC, ITV, and Channel 4, and a secondary school teacher.

Andrew Beck worked in UK secondary, further, and higher education for forty-two years, lastly as International Partnership Manager for Coventry University's Faculty of Arts and Humanities. He is author of best-selling and oft cited works such as Cultural Work and Communication Studies: The Essential Introduction, as well as having served as chief examiner for public and professional examinations. Retired from full-time work he continues to teach at and advise international universities, as well as researching and publishing on a range of media issues. Recent publications include contributions to books on Covid-19, the Ukraine war, Boris Johnson's premiership, as well as occasional features for China Eye.

Richard Lance Keeble is Professor of Journalism at the University of Lincoln, and Honorary Professor at Liverpool Hope University. He has written and edited 48 books on a wide range of media-related topics. In 2020, Routledge published a collection of his recent essays: on

George Orwell, literary journalism, war and peace reporting, and journalists and the secret state under the title Journalism Beyond Orwell. He is emeritus editor of Ethical Space: The International Journal of Communication Ethics which he launched in 2003, and joint editor of George Orwell Studies. From 2013 to 2020 he was chair of the Orwell Society. In 2011, he gained a National Teaching Fellowship, the highest award for teachers in higher education in the U.K., and in 2014 he was given a Lifetime Achievement Award by the Association for Journalism Education. He is a member of Louth Male Voice Choir, Louth Film Club, and (through thick and thin) Nottinghamshire County Cricket Club.

CONTENTS

Foreword   1
Sir Anthony Seldon, Headmaster, Epsom College

SECTION ONE
Royals managing the media

Introduction   3
John Mair

Chapter 1   7
Inside the royal box of tricks
Norman Baker, Former cabinet minister

Chapter 2   12
Constructing the royal media event: Pomp, populism, and King George V
Deborah David Wilson, Nottingham Trent University

Chapter 3   18
'Hello Big Ears': Reporting royalty in the provincial press
Carole O'Reilly, Salford University

Chapter 4   23
A reptile remembers
Martin Bell, Former BBC foreign correspondent

Chapter 5   27
Royal reporting: From deference to disgrace, and death in Paris
Michael Cole, Former BBC court correspondent

Chapter 6   32
Getting blood out of a royal stone
Charles Rae, Former royal correspondent, The Sun

Chapter 7   37
Reporting royalty: Janus journalism
Robin Aitken, The Daily Telegraph

Chapter 8   42
The missing years:
Prince Andrew, celebrity, and the media
Professor Jason Lee, De Montfort University

Chapter 9   48
The princes and the press:
nothing new here to see or hear
Michael Cole, Former BBC court correspondent

SECTION TWO
Courts and coronations

Introduction   51
Andrew Beck

Chapter 10   56
Harry goes to court
Liz Gerard, Former Times executive

Chapter 11   63
A sick relationship
Professor Julian Petley, Brunel University

Chapter 12   69
Don't mess with John Wayne or the royals:
The media, the law, and the royal family
Dr Steve Foster, Coventry University Law School

Chapter 13   74
Constructing royal soft power: A tabloid tradition
Dr Nathan Ritchie, Loughborough University

Chapter 14   79
Charles III's coronation on TV
John Mair

Chapter 15   84
King Charles III's coronation, a stylist's guide
Peter York, President, The Media Society

Chapter 16   87
All Perspectives?
Andrew Beck

Chapter 17   94
What the coronation papers say
Dr Alan Geere, Guangdong University of Foreign Studies

Chapter 18   101
Over there looking at over here (wistfully?)
Angela Antetomaso

Chapter 19   107
Do they mean us? How the international press reported Charles III's coronation
Raymond Snoddy, Former Times Media Editor

SECTION THREE
The end of the line?

Introduction   112
John Mair

Chapter 20   115
Some basic questions about the media and the monarchy
Sir Trevor Phillips, The Times

Chapter 21   118
Royal coverage: Not holding power to account
Marcus Ryder, Birmingham City University

Chapter 22   124
Standing at the coronation crossroads
Paul Connew, media commentator

Chapter 23   132
Irish republicanism and the monarchy
Dr Steven McCabe, Birmingham City University

Chapter 24   138
The Queen is dead; republic now!
Phil Butland, Die Linke Berlin

Afterword   144
From consensus to contention:
Changing public attitudes towards the monarchy
Professor Sir John Curtice, Strathclyde University

Foreword

Sir Anthony Seldon

Imagine Britain's monarchy without the media.
Impossible.
Imagine the popular media without the monarchy.
Bereft.
But still continuing to operate.
Was the monarchy always dependent on the media? Not before the 17th century, when the divine right of kings was the ruling orthodoxy. Henry VIII had no need to curry favour. Swish, swish. Off came the heads of queens and critics alike. Only from the 19th century, with the emergence of popular democracy, did things begin to change. Then, when the prime minister became a rival power to the monarch in the early 20th century, it forced the latter to think seriously about its public image.

That meant it had to cultivate the media big time. Popular newspapers began to take off in the 1920s, radio in the 1930s, public opinion polling in the 1940s, BBC television in the 1950s, and commercial television in the 1960s. Deference was over. The monarchy had to please, and to justify itself.

Welcome to today's symbiotic relationship. Like Philip Schofield and Holly Willoughby, the monarchy and the media might not like each other much, but needs must.

The last nine months have illustrated this pugilistic relationship in penetrating laser beams. The Queen's death, Harry, the Queen's Funeral, Harry, 'the book', Harry, the coronation, Penny, Harry.

Perfect time that for a bite-sized book to make sense of the monarchy and the media, bringing together journalists, academics, and a sprinkling of recovering insiders. At last, illumination from this galaxy of diverse perspectives. Who is playing whom? Who is poacher, and who gamekeeper?

There's no point in the royals complaining about the media. It's like sounding off about rain, which is as predictable: the royals have to get over it. Whether they were born into it, or marry into it, there are rules that have to be followed. Rules number one to ten: any sense of entitlement is a catastrophe. Margaret, Andrew, Harry... The country owes the royal family nothing. The nation's love and support have to be earned, by its service, leadership, and good example.

The women generally understand this better. The Queen Mother, the late Queen, Princess Anne, the Duchess of Edinburgh, and Camilla. And Queen among Queens, Kate.

Kate plays the media to perfection. Unlike Diana, there's total poise and command, no victimhood. There's something very knowing about her. She and William bolster each other's strengths, the polar opposites of Harry and Meghan magnifying each other's weaknesses and insecurities.

Camilla too gets it, far more than Charles. She's savvy, predictable, and not needy. As Charles ages, she'll become increasingly dominant, a master craftsman sculpting and defining the Carolean Age.

With Andrew banished, Meghan and Harry empty of further accusations, and young George waiting in the wings to make the succession secure deep into the 22nd century, what could possibly go wrong?

Public opinion. With more 18-24-year-olds favouring an elected head of state over the royal family, the skates could be under the monarchy unless the numbers improve. Because the media are only friendly to the monarchy in as far as readers and viewers support it. The continuation of the royal family as head of state is a live issue in the only 14 remaining countries left in the Commonwealth following Barbados' abandonment of it in 2021. Surely it's only a matter of time before Australia parts with the monarchy: its media is notably cool to it compared with the British media.

Monarchy after monarchy worldwide clattered out of existence in the 19th and 20th centuries. Now only 40 remain. The direction of travel is indisputable.

There will always be a media. There might not always be a monarchy.

About the contributor

Sir Anthony Seldon is headmaster of Epsom College, and was previously head of Brighton and Wellington Colleges. He is one of Britain's foremost historians. His latest book Johnson at 10: The Inside Story (Atlantic Books), an account of Boris Johnson's turbulent time as UK Prime Minister, was a 2023 non-fiction highlight of both The Times and The Observer, and a Sunday Times instant best-seller.

SECTION ONE
Royals managing the media

Introduction
John Mair

This book explores near virgin territory: the relationship between the British royal family and the British media. Healthy? Reporting or mere tittle-tattle? Two out-of-date institutions supporting each other like two drunken men after a good night out? The question is a complicated one. Royalty sells newspapers and attracts TV audiences, but whilst the royals can and do manage the media they are also deeply distrustful of it. That fragile peace sometimes breaks down as with the Duke and Duchess of Sussex's seemingly unending legal war against the popular press. 'Never apologise, sue if need be' is the Montecito take on the usual Windsor media formula of 'Never explain, never apologise'. Skirmishes in their war are now almost weekly occurrences, the battlefield being the High Court in the Strand. Harry and Meghan keep Schillings, their lawyers, well provided with briefs. The first section of this book looks at the history of the hack-royal relationship.

There are twenty-five crisply written chapters in this volume. Produced by hacks and academics, the vast majority of them were written especially for this book. The first piece is one of the few exceptions. Norman Baker was a minister in the 2010-2015 Tory/Liberal Democrat coalition. He is now the prime standard bearer for British republicanism, the Willie Hamilton MP de nos jours. In this short extract from his 2019 book And What Do You Do? — What The Royal Family Don't Want You To Know he looks at the past and present of British royalty and the media. 'Inside the royal box of tricks' examines royal media manipulation in the reigns of George III, Victoria, George V, George VI, and Elizabeth II. He returns to the 1930s and the pro-Nazi sentiments of the Duke of Windsor and how that has been either 'forgotten' or buried. He concludes, 'Perhaps most egregious has been the way in which the clear pro-fascist and pro-appeasement views of the royal family in the 1930s and into the 1940s have been cleaned up or airbrushed out'.

Deborah Wilson David is now a journalism academic but was a radio producer. She details the growth of the love/hate relationship between Buckingham Palace and the electronic media. King Charles III's May 2023 coronation was covered effectively by up to 200 live television cameras and became in essence a made-for-television event. Compare and contrast. In 'Constructing the royal media event: Pomp, populism, and King George V' she recalls, 'In 1937, three television cameras stationed at Hyde Park Corner broadcast the pictures live to ten thousand. For King Charles III's May 2023, coronation an audience of more than 20 million in the UK, and many more millions worldwide, watched the ceremony live'.

Dr Carole O'Reilly of Salford University looks at the grass roots of journalism —local papers — and their royal reporting. In 'Hello Big Ears: Reporting royalty in the provincial press' she explains how the royal visit is too often reported in hushed tones by the local press. Princess Diana was their black and white heroine - she was glam and sold papers - and there are signs today of the return of that template with Kate, Princess of Wales. O'Reilly observes, 'It is striking that very similar words are still used about Catherine in the local press that were applied to her late mother-in-law: 'compassionate', 'radiant', and there is a similar focus on her fashion choices'.

From the local to two big beasts (retired) of the television journalism world. Martin Bell and Michael Cole were kings of the BBC News jungle in their era. Bell, who later became an independent MP, did his fair share on the royal beat especially whilst with the royal circus on tour. In 'A reptile remembers' he recalls how he and other bored journalists invented games to lessen the gruel and grind of a royal tour, 'At the Commonwealth Heads of Government Conference in Cyprus in 1993 a well-known TV reporter was challenged by a colleague to introduce the phrase 'Phil the Greek' [the then Duke of Edinburgh] into one of his scripts. 'The arrival of the Queen and the Duke,' he wrote, 'will fill the Greeks with pride'. He won the bet'.

Michael Cole was king of the TV royal roost for many years. In 1987 he took an off-the-record lunch with print colleagues at face value. Cole indicated in general terms what the Queen would say in her recorded Christmas broadcast. Two of those colleagues put these comments on the record. The BBC suffered, and Cole was sent to the salt mines of media and arts for ten months before resigning to join Harrods. In a very thoughtful piece, 'Royal reporting: from deference to disgrace, and death in Paris', he reverts to the classic work on the British Constitution: 'Were the great 19th century constitutional writer Walter Bagehot around today, he would not be warning against letting light in upon the magic of monarchy. It's too late for that. Rather, Bagehot would be advising that decency, honesty, and plain dealing should both shape the relationship between King Charles III and the media because a constitutional monarchy suits the British temperament in many ways. Its demise would be a loss to both sovereign and his subjects'.

British (and world) tabloids feast on the British monarchy: rifts, family rows, rumours (true or false), and tittle-tattle their stock in trade. Harry and Meghan and their divorce from 'The Firm' represent copy manna for them. Charlie Rae pounded the TODAY and Sun royal beats for many years. In those days there was a strong esprit de royal press corps. In the words of John Mortimer ,'We may not be the creme de la creme, but we are the creme de la scum'. In 'Getting blood out of a royal stone', Rae a hard-bitten Scottish hack, is unequivocal in how he sees the subject of his stories: 'I have always regarded the royal family as one huge real-life soap where many scriptwriters would find some of the plots even too outrageous for television. But it is a fascinating subject, and it is the gift that keeps on giving to journalists'. For which the tabloids give thanks.

Even to the Conservative not-so-popular press. Robin Aitken of the Daily Telegraph, ex-BBC, is an unreconstructed social conservative. In 'Reporting royalty: Janus journalism' he is coruscating, yet sympathetic, to the current BBC coverage of the royals. His view is that, 'Since the Bashir affair [the 1995 Princess Diana Panorama interview obtained through dubious methods] the BBC has been conspicuously, one might almost say unctuously, loyal in its royal coverage; perhaps in subconscious expiation for its sins'.

Like other families, the Windsors seem to have a share of black sheep. Prince Andrew is the most egregious example. Mutating from 'Randy Andy' to (alleged) 'Paedo Andy' in a decade through an ill-judged relationship with convicted sex offender Jeffrey Epstein, and an even more ill-judged attempt to justify it in a disastrous 2019 Newsnight interview, he has firmly put himself firmly beyond the royal pale. Stripped of royal and military titles and even his tied house. In 'The missing years: Prince Andrew, celebrity, and the media' Professor Jason Lee of De Montfort University looks at the omerta in the British media over the years on the unsavoury activities of the Duke of York and other 'child abusers'. Lee spent years trying to break this academic and journalistic silence until Newsnight did.. He concludes, 'Academic presses were also uninterested in Prince Andrew's case from fear of being sued. Only when Prince Andrew decided to do an interview, erroneously attempting to kill the story, did media discourse surrounding child sexual abuse in a royal context advance'.

Finally in this section, back to the doyen: Michael Cole, ex-BBC, and ex-PR for Mohamed Al Fayed and his campaign to clear the name of his son from being blamed for the death of Princess Diana in the Pont de l'Alma tunnel in Paris in 1997. Ultimately that effort failed. Cole sums up the interdependence of the royal-reptile relationship in 'The princes and the press'. There he concludes, 'The truth is the monarchy suits the British temperament and relies on the Press, TV, and radio to maintain its relationship with the people. The time for the monarchy to worry would be when the media were no longer interested. That would mean the show was over'.

So the relationship is impure and unhealthy but is also vital for both sides of this marriage of convenience.

Chapter 1

Inside the royal box of tricks

In his 2019 analysis of the British royal family's relationship with the media **Norman Baker** identified five tricks they employ to maintain their positive public image: (1) the use of spin doctors, (2) control of photographs and photo opportunities, (3) removing access for journalists and media unwilling to toe the royal line, (4) threats of legal action, and (5) the construction of a fog of secrecy

It was George III who appointed the first spin doctor, around two hundred years before Tony Blair and Alastair Campbell made the phrase common currency. The King had become irritated by generally accurate newspaper stories about his activities, and decided a counterbalance was required. So a 'Court Newsman' was appointed, and given the task of distributing daily to the press information about royal engagements. It was called the Court Circular, and can still be found tucked away somewhere in The Times, and now also on the Palace website.

Come the age of photography, and it did not take the royals long to work out that photographs of themselves were useful in consolidating support. The first family photo appeared in 1857, and five years later one taken of the Prince of Wales and his bride Alexandra sold a staggering two million copies.

Between that year and her death in 1901, Queen Victoria registered 428 official portraits for sale. They appeared everywhere, including on household products like toilet soap. The use of royal images continues unabated to the present day, except nowadays the purveyors are largely newspapers and other media. The Palace, which sternly argues that royal children should be protected from press intrusion, is nevertheless quite content to make available photographs of them on special occasions such as birthdays.

The pictures are invariably used, and prominently in the tabloids in particular, for the simple reason that the editors believe – with good reason – that such pictures sell papers. But it is an uncomfortable deal for the press. It is the Palace that controls the supply of pictures, both in timing and content. Naturally only those which show the image the Palace wants to convey are made available. They are, in effect, securing space in the papers for their message, just like an advertiser, except in this case, the space comes free, and indeed with a supportive editorial line.

A normal, happy family

Down the decades, official pictures have been used to reinforce the notion of the royals as a normal, happy family. The truth has been somewhat different. Unlike in most families, royal children – especially the Queen's – have often been left with nannies for months on end while their parents are abroad. Prince Philip managed to miss all of his son Charles's first five birthdays. And when the young Charles was rushed to hospital for an emergency appendectomy at midnight, the Queen stayed tucked up in her bed. When Anne, at a tender age, had her tonsils removed, it was nanny who stayed with her in hospital overnight, while her mother remained in Windsor Castle.

Nor do the seemingly normal family photos which are made public always reflect reality. You would not guess, for example, from the early photographs of Charles with his parents that the rules of the house meant that he always had to bow to his mum before he left the room.

Of course, on the occasions that the press publishes photographs that the Palace does not want the public to see, they protest in vigorous terms, such as when in 2015 The Sun published pre-war pictures of a young Elizabeth and the future Queen Mother giving a Nazi salute, egged on by the future Edward VIII.

One early example of spin came in 1936 with the death of George V. At 11 pm on 20 January, he was injected with fatal doses of morphine and cocaine. Death would certainly have happened within days at most, probably hours, but it was brought forward in order that this would, according to the notes of the royal physician Lord Dawson, appear 'in the morning papers rather than the less appropriate evening journals'. At 10 pm, the physician arranged for The Times to be tipped off that the King would die that evening, and they held back publication accordingly. George V was not consulted about this medical intervention. Legally speaking, Lord Dawson committed murder, and indeed treason, to secure what he deemed the appropriate newspaper coverage, although it might well be argued that his actions also prevented unnecessary suffering. In a House of Lords debate later that year, he called such interventions a 'mission of mercy'.

Addicted to spin

Patrick Jephson, who was private secretary to Diana, warned in 2017 that the royal family's addiction to spin was dangerous for them:

> We forgive politicians their spin doctors [...] because we can vote them in or out. But if your purpose constitutionally is to be a unifying force, a symbol of continuity [...] then you are on thin ice. What we have now is a determination to control the message, to control the image.

He accused the Palace, as Diana split from Charles, of spreading a 'vile diagnosis that she had a clinical personality disorder, a slur then systematically spread by royal spin doctors and still whispered to this day'. The raw truth about the state of the marriage between Charles and Diana was that much more shocking when it finally emerged precisely because the public had been sold the union as a sort of royal fairy tale.

Linked with this is another trick in the royal box: downgrade or remove access for those journalists or media outlets who do not behave as the Palace wants. After the famous 1995 BBC Panorama episode where Diana sensationally talked of there being three people in her marriage, the Palace responded by giving ITV pole position for the Queen's next Christmas message.

Just because there is interest from the public in a particular matter, this does not make it a matter of public interest. The problem comes when the threat or indeed instigation of legal action is used, not to protect a genuinely private matter, but to prevent the public from learning something which they are entitled to know, but which the royals wish to hush up because it is embarrassing.

The royal family has overall become far more willing to resort to legal action than it was in the past, and does not seem to distinguish between cases which represent a genuine invasion of privacy, and cases where it is simply that they would rather a particular story did not appear.

In 2015, a BBC documentary 'Reinventing the Royals' was delayed at the last moment after the corporation received a warning letter from Harbottle & Lewis. Clarence House had originally given the green light, but developed cold feet when it appeared the programme might actually be a proper piece of research rather than the hagiography for

Charles they had assumed was on its way. The BBC to its credit did broadcast the two-parter a few weeks later.

The fog of secrecy

But it is the last trick in the royal box that is the most powerful, and the most sinister. It is the fog of secrecy with which they have managed to envelop themselves, and inside that fog to behave in ways they simply would not dare if the public knew what they were doing, or to lock away records of the past which they do not wish to see the light of day, even to pervert and destroy our history where it suits them to do so.

In the 19th century, entire records from three centuries earlier were destroyed because they reflected adversely on the private life of Edward I. Similarly Edward VII left instructions that all his letters were to be burnt, and the same fate befell a painting of George V that its subject did not like.

Perhaps most egregious has been the way in which the clear pro-fascist and pro-appeasement views of the royal family in the 1930s and into the 1940s have been cleaned up or airbrushed out. At the end of the war, many embarrassing documents, revealing the pro-Nazi views of many in the royal family and the wider British Establishment, ended up in the hands of the new civilian German government, or the American forces. Anthony Blunt, later uncloaked as a Russian spy, was repeatedly sent to Germany on the orders of George VI to retrieve all the damaging material he could so that it might be destroyed.

Clement Attlee's new Labour government had been only too keen to exploit Nazi files that they now had in their possession, but changed their mind when faced with the problem of incriminating royal material. A batch entitled the 'Windsor File' was regarded as particularly sensitive. This contained comments of the Duke of Windsor while he was on the continent and which found their way at the time into German intelligence. Two copies of the file now held by the civilian German government had been made, one being handed to London and one to the Americans. Securing the return to Britain of the American copy, or its destruction by them, became a major objective of British foreign policy at this time, and a good deal of scarce political capital was expended on it in Britain's engagement with the Americans, who became irritated with this British obsession.

The State Department's Director of European Affairs, John Hickerson, wrote in a top-secret message that he expected the British government to resist strongly the publication of any material relating to the Duke of Windsor. 'There is throughout the United Kingdom an unreasoning devotion to the monarchical principle and an almost fanatical disposition to do everything possible to protect the good name of the institution of the monarchy.'

One of the reasons the Queen's time in office was a success was because we did not officially know what she thought on most issues, although we could have probably make a shrewd assessment. Studious, conscientious and boring is what is required and what she has broadly delivered.

Prince Charles has chosen a different route from his mother, and therein lies danger for the monarchy. If as king he is seen as simply another politician, support for the monarchy will soon ebb away. As The Times acidly put it in an editorial, 'a head of state with an opinion is called a president, not a prince'.

This chapter is extracted from Norman Baker's book And What Do You Do? — What The Royal Family Don't Want You To Know. The editors offer their grateful thanks to both him and his publisher, Biteback Publishing, for permission to reproduce this extract.

About the contributor

Norman Baker was Liberal Democrat MP for Lewes, East Sussex from 1997 to 2015. He served in the 2010-2015 UK coalition government, first as Parliamentary Under-Secretary of State in the Department of Transport, and then as Minister of State at the Home Office. He has published three books: The Strange Death of David Kelly (2007), Against the Grain (2015), and And What Do You Do? — What The Royal Family Don't Want You To Know (2019).

Chapter 2

Constructing the royal media event: Pomp, populism, and King George V

Tracing the origins of the relationship between royalty and the BBC, **Deborah Wilson David** looks at Lord Reith's persistence in securing King George V's engagement with the emerging medium, and how the establishment of royal media events aligned with his aspirations for the BBC

Queen Victoria's Diamond Jubilee procession in 1897 was the first royal event to be captured on film and shared with a wider audience. However, this event was not simply a celebration of the Queen's reign, but also a powerful demonstration of the emerging technology of motion pictures. Film would play a significant role in shaping the future of the British monarchy's relationship with the public and construct a carefully crafted image of the monarchy for mass consumption. It was just one year after moving pictures were first seen publicly in Britain, and forty cameramen from twenty film companies covered the route by taking short films of the parade from Buckingham Palace to St Paul's Cathedral.

The use of film to capture and disseminate images of the procession was an exercise in spectacle and served to create a carefully curated image of the monarchy as a grand and powerful institution, paving the way for a new era in which royal events could be captured on film and disseminated to a wider audience. As McKernan claims, it was a display of Empire and global authority: 'Queen Victoria's Diamond Jubilee was the first true example of that increasingly common phenomenon of the past 115 years, the media event' (McKernan 2012:2).

By 1901, the film industry had experienced significant advancements in technology, and the funeral of Queen Victoria was documented on film and made available for public viewing. This served as a template for the royal funerals to follow.

Along comes the BBC

But it was in the reign of Queen Victoria's grandson that broadcasting, with the launch of the British Broadcasting Company in 1922, began in the UK. King George V was mid-reign when the BBC launched and John Reith, the newly appointed General Manager, began a determined campaign to seek the royal seal of approval for his endeavours.

The wireless was a growing medium globally and although Reith would be the last to be impressed by American broadcasting, he could not have been unaware that presidents of the United States were pioneers in using the airwaves effectively: firstly Warren G Harding in 1922 and then Calvin Coolidge with his first State of the Union address to 23 million listeners in December 1923. President Coolidge would go on to quickly embrace radio and become a successful radio communicator and radio personality (Bittinger in Wallace 2008: vi).

Perhaps inspired by this, Reith approached the King in 1923 to ask if he would be willing to broadcast to his people on a significant holiday such as Christmas, New Year, or Easter: 'Unfortunately, the King was a reluctant speech-giver – due to a self-perceived lack of oral talent – and also an unashamed technophobe. He politely declined this request, much to the BBC's disappointment' (Glencross 2013).

A first royal speech

The King agreed to accept a wireless set that year, which was some form of recognition of the fledgling medium, but it did not appear to have the immediate effect of persuading him to make any personal addresses in the way Reith was seeking. However, the following year the King's voice was heard — and the recording is now held at by the British Library, notable as the first royal broadcast made on radio and the earliest surviving recording of any radio broadcast (Howells 2022). When microphones captured the King's opening address at the British Empire Exhibition at Wembley Park in April 1924 Reith was pleased: 'Everything went most successfully, including the broadcast which went out all over the country and was the biggest thing we have done yet' (Reith in Stuart 1975: 133).

And this was not the only function at which the King's announcements were transmitted via the wireless. These broadcasts were popular with the listeners, but still the King remained unconvinced that he should give a personal message to the population on Christmas Day or in any other respect. Reith noted in his diaries his irritation at the royal reticence: 'It is quite extraordinary how conservative they are' (Reith in Stuart 1975: 182).

Further pressure was gently applied by Ramsay MacDonald, the Labour Prime Minister. He attempted to assuage many of the King's fears about a personal broadcast, saying that a simple, honest approach would be more than adequate for the task, that the monarchy was pivotal for maintaining national unity. The Prime Minister suggested that Rudyard Kipling could write the speech, thus relieving the King of another anxiety (Day 2021).

Breaking the silence

Reith's diaries show that the combination of the launch of the BBC's Empire Service in mid-December 1932, plus 'a strong recommendation from the prime minister' (Reith in Stuart 1975: 183), finally persuaded the King to give the first Christmas Day address.

Hendy notes that despite the King taking some persuading he achieved precisely what Reith had been seeking, the head of one family speaking to the millions of others 'almost as if in that single instant broadcasting symbolically bound together as one "the family audience, the royal family, the nation as family"'. Reith was delighted with the result: 'Nothing went wrong; all excellent. The King's message impressive and moving beyond expectation. It was a triumph for him and for BBC engineers and programme planners' (Reith 1949: 168). The reaction to the broadcast was very positive, which left the King 'very pleased and much moved' (BBC 2023).

Reith had certainly believed that broadcasting had brought King and country together in times of both war and peace: 'it had brought the solicitude of fatherhood in where before was the aloof dignity of the throne' (Reith in Stuart 1975: 184). He saw the BBC as a unifying force — and the monarchy part of the armoury to help with that unification. Reith cited this speech by George V as a particular success in this regard (Scannell and Cardiff, 1991: 278).

Radio funeral

King George V died in January 1936. His declining health had been reported in radio bulletins from January 15: 'Official announcement from Sandringham broadcast in the News that the King had a cold due to the severe wintry weather, and was confined to his room' (Hibberd 1950:124). Arrangements were made for announcers to be available on shift to broadcast bulletins over the weekend. On the evening of 20 January, the BBC's domestic and short-wave Empire Service outputs were brought together and a bulletin from Sandringham that 'the King's life is moving peacefully towards its close' was repeated every quarter of the hour through the late evening by chief announcer Stuart Hibberd, with normal programmes suspended until Reith made the final announcement at a quarter past midnight that the King had died. And for the first time, millions of people received the news of the passing of the Sovereign at the same time.

Showreel footage took the funeral to the wider public after the event — but for the first time, there was live coverage — on BBC radio. Cancellation of normal programming, substituting others more appropriate, the broadcasts of the funeral procession through London and of the funeral service at St George's Chapel Windsor were all part of the coverage of the first royal death the BBC had to manage (Reith 1949: 241).

After the King's death in 1936, Wigram wrote to Reith saying, 'King George was a Victorian, but he was beginning to realise the wonders of broadcasting, and what a link this was between him and his peoples [...] There is no doubt that one of the great events of his reign was broadcasting, which made him the great king that he was' (Reith 1949: 240-241).

One king exits on radio; another enters

The BBC was given the responsibility for relaying Edward VIII's abdication speech in 1936, with John Reith personally attending, indeed welcoming the short-reigning King to Windsor Castle, described vividly in his autobiography Into the Wind (Reith 1949: 266-269).

Then in May 1937, came King George VI's coronation, the first coronation to be broadcast.

Thirty-eight microphones were placed inside Westminster Abbey and twenty outside. The new King had rehearsed his speech on a closed circuit in the Palace, studying the playbacks to get the best speed, inflexion and tone: 'A gramophone record of the speech as delivered during the final rehearsal was ready as a standby in case anything went wrong' (Reith 1949: 280).

It was the first major outside broadcast in the early, experimental, days of television. No television cameras were permitted in the Abbey, but the procession was televised from Hyde Park Corner (McIntyre

1993: 230) and the event prompted the purchase of 9,000 television sets in the London area (National Science and Media Museum).

Briggs argues that, 'It has often and rightly been argued that the practice of royal broadcasting lent a new dimension to constitutional monarchy' (Briggs 1961: 290). Over succeeding years, the sophistication of the coverage increased in line with the attention given to the detail of the events themselves. Planning for royal weddings, funerals, and now of course the first coronation in the UK 70 years, have developed apace. In 1937, three television cameras stationed at Hyde Park Corner broadcast the pictures live to ten thousand homes. For King Charles III's May 2023 coronation, an audience of more than 20 million in the UK, and many more millions worldwide, watched the ceremony live.

References

BBC https://www.bbc.com/historyofthebbc/anniversaries/december/christmas-message Accessed 1 May 2023

Cyndy Bittinger (2008) 'Radio President', in Jerry L Wallace (2008) Calvin Coolidge Our First Radio President, Vermont: Five Corners Press.

Asa Briggs (1961) The History of Broadcasting the United Kingdom Volume 1 The Birth of Broadcasting, London: Oxford University Press.

Joel Day, 24 Dec 2021, the Express https://www.express.co.uk/news/royal/1540567/king-george-v-thwarted-christmas-speech-queens-speech-royal-family-spt Accessed 1 May 2023

Matthew Glencross (24 April 2013) https://history.blog.gov.uk/2013/04/24/the-first-christmas-speech/ Accessed 1 May 2023

Stuart Hibberd (1950) This — is London..., Bungay: Richard Clay and Company Ltd.

Katherine Howells (2022) 'A vast window display': The British Empire Exhibition of 1924-25 https://blog.nationalarchives.gov.uk/20speople-a-vast-window-display-the-british-empire-exhibition-of-1924-5/ Accessed 1 May 2023

Marista Leishman (2006) My Father — Reith of the BBC, Edinburgh: Saint Andrew Press.

Ian McIntyre (1993) The Expense of Glory, A Life of John Reith, London: HarperCollins.

Luke McKernan (2012) Queen Victoria's Diamond Jubilee http://lukemckernan.com/wp-content/uploads/queen_victoria_diamond_jubilee.pdf Accessed 1 May 2023

National Science and Media Museum https://blog.scienceandmediamuseum.org.uk/history-of-british-television-timeline/ Accessed 1 May 2023

JCW Reith (1949) Into The Wind, London: Hodder & Stoughton.
Paddy Scannell and David Cardiff (1991) A Social History of British Broadcasting, Volume One 1922 – 1939 Serving the Nation, Oxford: Basil Blackwell Ltd.
Charles Stuart (ed) (1975) The Reith Diaries, London: Collins

About the contributor

Deborah Wilson David is head of the Department of Journalism and Media at Nottingham Trent University. An early adopter of hackademic work practices, she has combined broadcasting and education for 30 years. Her research interests focus on the history of broadcasting, particularly the establishment of the BBC, the reporting of World War II, and BBC local radio. She sits on the Board of the US-based Broadcast Education Association, representing the Association's International membership, and served for six years as the Vice President of the European Journalism Training Association.

Chapter 3

'Hello Big Ears': Reporting royalty in the provincial press

The provincial press and the British royal family have long had an ambivalent relationship. Who has benefited most from this relationship and why? **Carole O'Reilly** *investigates the portrayal of various family members in selections from local newspapers since the 1953 coronation of Queen Elizabeth II*

Most of the national press (with the exception of The Guardian and, initially, The Independent) have maintained their positive, nay subservient, royal coverage, but how have the royals fared in the local press? It was a reporter from the Bradford Telegraph and Argus who broke the story of King Edward VIII's affair with Mrs Simpson in 1936 (Priestley 2006). Ever since, the local and regional press has reported on the royal family in ways that both supplemented and challenged their national counterparts.

Covering the patch from both sides

The reasons for a royal visit to provincial towns and cities was usually linked to some local event. Clever public relations was an early mark of the royal family's awareness of their local appeal. The Queen Mother, on a visit to York in 1954, wore a spray of white roses on her coat and a hat with a white rose (the symbol of Yorkshire). A similar tactic was used for a visit to Sunderland by Princess Diana in 1985 when she was dressed 'head to toe in Sunderland's soccer colours – red and white' (Newcastle Journal, 22 May 1985).

The attributes of the county or region were often reflected in the local reporting. Visits by the royals to Yorkshire often elicited references to 'homeliness' and a 'homely welcome', while the teenage Princess Anne was referred to as a 'swinging hinny', honey in the local dialect by the Newcastle Journal on a visit in 1969 (3 May).

The family members' rapport with local people (especially children) and places was emphasised and any local links were amplified. The Queen directly referred to the royal family's connections to Hull Docks during a 1969 visit. Local dissent was often mentioned as well. Some vocal protesters greeted Prince Charles and Princess Diana in Sunderland in 1985 with posters reading, 'Hello Big Ears', 'Hello Fertile Missie', and 'Parasites Go Home'. The paper's reaction to the demonstrators was fairly negative with a front-page headline asking, 'Royal demo: how could it happen?' An editorial apologised to the royal couple and referred to the protesters as 'misguided oafs' (Newcastle Journal, 22 May 1985).

Recently, protests by the anti-monarchy group Republic have accompanied King Charles and his consort on local visits to cities such as Milton Keynes and Colchester in 2023. These have been reported without editorial comment. A Daily Gazette report on the Colchester visit noted that it had cost taxpayers £6000 (5 April 2023) while the same paper had printed a positive account of the visit the previous month (8 March 2023). This continuing ambivalence represents an attempt to appeal to both pro-and anti-monarchist readers as well as to reflect a public opinion that is apparently more lukewarm about the monarchy (Hill 2023).

The role of photography

One of the most common methods of recording the details of royal visits to a locality was by the publication of photographs. These often took the form of a special supplement published by a newspaper to celebrate the occasion. At times, this could be purely seen as a commercial venture: in 1998 the Grimsby Evening Telegraph published a 4-page supplement to commemorate the tenth anniversary of a visit to the town by Princess Diana in 1988. Taking advantage of the continuing public mourning for the late Princess, the paper used the opportunity to boost sales by offering a photographic reminder of the Princess's trip.

Many local visit reports were totally dominated by several pages of photos, especially those undertaken by Diana. Her 1992 visit to Hull was celebrated by an eight-page souvenir special, while in Liverpool in 1990 eight photos of her featured on a single page. Diana's photogenic appeal was obvious but these supplements also had a commercial motive: boosting local press sales in a competitive era and attempting to compete with glossy celebrity-focused magazines such as Hello! which launched in Britain in 1988.

Royal visits were almost always front-page news for the local press, taking full advantage of the opportunity to print large, eye-catching photos. Looking over the history of such photos and their use, we can note the tendency to use full-length photos of royal women more than men, dating back to the 1950s and the emphasis on using facial close-ups of the female family members which accelerated with Diana. More recently, this trend has continued with Catherine and Meghan, with the addition of video footage of their visits on local newspapers' websites.

Royal women's dress sense

There is little doubt that general press coverage of the royal family changed with the arrival of Princess Diana in 1980, as Blain and O'Donnell have commented 'no-one in history was so much a product of the media as Diana and no-one was ever more governed by her own image' (Blain and O'Donnell, 2003: 172). But, did she take the local press in a new direction entirely or did she merely accentuate trends and tendencies that already existed?

Coverage of female members of the royal family was already more positive in the decades preceding Diana's arrival. In fact, a good deal of the coverage of royal women tended more toward the emotional rather than the factual. The Queen Mother's 'friendly informality' was often commented on during royal visits in the 1950s, while there were 'gasps of admiration' for Princess Anne's dress on a visit to Hull in 1969. The report on the latter included four paragraphs on the fashions of both Anne and her mother, the Queen, with just one sentence reserved for the Duke of Edinburgh's attire (Hull Daily Mail, 4 August 1969).

Much of the commentary on royal women revolved around their dress and fashion sense as well as their physique. Sarah Ferguson was described as 'fun', 'talkative', and 'slimline' (this in the context of her very public struggles with her weight) on successive visits to Salford in 1989 and 1991. Words such as 'fairy tale' and 'radiant' were most commonly used in reference to Diana, as well as 'caring' and 'compassionate'. A visit to Liverpool in 1990 described her 'special brand of magic with children' (Liverpool Echo, 12 September 1990), while a visit to Hull in 1992 evoked the comment that 'when she left, there was hardly a dry eye in the house' (Hull Daily Mail, 8 June 1992).

Behind the dresses

The levels of emotive reporting increased yet further with the emergence of the difficulties in the Wales's marriage. Then Diana was described as 'wearing the mask of the professional' in Hull in 1992 and as 'tearful' in Preston in 1993. The failure of the ultimate fairy tale marriage enabled a new and more ambivalent style of commentary on the royals which continued to value their commitment to local visits while acknowledging that these often came at a personal cost.

This was often a reflection of the amount of sympathy directed at Diana in particular by the general public. A visit to Hull by Diana in 1992 prompted local journalist Jo Davidson to recognise the difficulties of having her marriage 'dissected as thoroughly and as cruelly as a rat in a science lab' but also to wonder at her motives, noting a 'hint of triumph in those massive blue eyes' (Hull Daily Mail, 25 June 1992). This level of awareness of Diana's alleged manipulative relationship with the press was by no means universal in the local papers but there was a growing consciousness among local journalists that the disintegration of the marriage was a good basis for scrutiny of the couple in the context of local visits and tours and that such analysis was not just acceptable but of some commercial value.

Similar ambivalence was also on display about Prince Charles during a visit to Liverpool in 1984. The reporter noted that he was a 'likeable, dutiful chap' but alluded to rumours about his boredom with his role and conflict with his father. The article called for the Prince to 'treasure and value' local people's positive response to him (Liverpool Echo, 17 October 1984).

Next in line . . .

While Pat Robins has claimed that 'a happy Royal marriage is not good press' (1995: 114), there is some evidence that coverage of local visits by Prince William and Princess Catherine have re-established a template of a happy royal relationship. It is striking that very similar words are still used about Catherine in the local press that were applied to her late mother-in-law: 'compassionate', 'radiant', and there is a similar focus on her fashion choices. There is less emphasis on the local aspects of the visits in these more recent reports, reflecting a less locally focused press that is often centrally based and edited. This content is designed to be shared among a number of regional hubs so the local lens has become less significant.

Think local

The provincial press has sought to both document royal visits and to reflect public opinion about the royals more generally. Patterns of coverage vary according to contemporary attitudes but with a tacit acknowledgement of the continuing commercial appeal of some royal family members in a local context. Future trends in the wake of the death of Queen Elizabeth will be interesting to observe for a more sceptical public and a provincial press that is progressively less focused on the local.

References

Neil Blain and Hugh O'Donnell (2003) Media, Monarchy and Power, Bristol: Intellect Books.
Amelia Hill (2023) 'British public support for monarchy at historic low, poll reveals', Guardian, 28 April. Available online at: https://www.theguardian.com/uk-news/2023/apr/28/public-support-monarchy-historic-low-poll-reveals
Mike Priestley (2006) 'Not-so-blunt words that stopped Coronation', Telegraph and Argus, 1 December. Available online at: https://www.thetelegraphandargus.co.uk/news/1053791.not-so-blunt-words-that-stopped-coronation/
Pat Robins (1995) 'Media Representations of the British Royal Family as National Family', European Journal of Women's Studies, Vol. 2, No. 1, pp 113-116

About the contributor

Carole O'Reilly is Senior Lecturer in Media and Cultural Studies at the University of Salford. She received her PhD in History from Manchester Metropolitan University in 2009. She has published widely on the social and cultural history of the press, including the co-authored book, Newspaper Building Design and Journalism Cultures in Australia and the UK, 1855-2010 (Routledge, 2022). She has appeared on Great British Railway Journeys, and her work has been published in academic journals such as Media History and in popular magazines such as History Today and History Revealed.

Chapter 4

A reptile remembers

Distinguished veteran BBC correspondent
Martin Bell *recalls his royal encounters*

Achieving high office by birth and not by election, the royal family is by its very nature hierarchical and undemocratic. Yet it depends for its survival on the support of the people. Without that its principal figures are merely wealthy and entitled characters living in big houses, liable to be swept into history at the drop of a referendum.

To connect them, whether they like it or not — and often they do not — they need the mediation of the press, also known to them and ourselves as the 'reptiles'. And yes, among other and more dangerous assignments, I too was a sometime reptile.

My reptile history

As an apprentice reptile I reported the Investiture of the Prince of Wales at Caernarvon Castle in 1969, and later his tour of Canada, with Princess Diana. As a more mature reptile, I reported the Queen in The Seychelles, at a Kentucky horse farm, on the West Coast of the United States with Ronald Reagan, and in the Caribbean from Jamaica to the Cayman Islands. We were not allowed to interview her, but we could accost her husband. At a wild-life reserve in the Caymans I summoned up the courage to ask the Duke of Edinburgh why he was in favour of preserving wild-life abroad while shooting it at home. He gave no answer, but his look alone could have sent me to the Tower. Royal reporting, like war reporting, needs steadiness under fire.

Of these excursions the most remarkable was Charles and Diana's nineteen-day tour of Canada in June 1983, billed as a honeymoon event, although the one-year-old Prince William was left at home, to the evident dismay of his mother. They crossed the country from coast to coast, with never a visitors' book unsigned or a ceremonial tree unplanted. It was a premonition of things to come that she was cheered to the echo and he was not. By way of entertainment they were obliged to listen to a drunken speech by the Premier of Nova Scotia. By the time they reached Prince Edward Island I was so bored that I wrote my closing script in rhyming couplets and iambic pentameters – and no one even noticed!

The reptile pack

The press corps at the time were a raffish bunch, back in the great and glory days of Fleet Street. They included James Whitaker, then of the Mirror, billed as 'the man who really knows the royals', who had a talent for inserting himself at the centre of the story and appearing to be as at least as important as they were. His friend and rival was Harry Arnold of The Sun, who remarked of the press corps, after John Mortimer, that, 'They call us the scum, but at least we are the crème de la crème of the scum'. And there was an ingenious photographer who hit upon the idea of wearing a hat with a stuffed pigeon stitched into it, so that wherever Diana went she looked directly at him, which gave him the picture of the day. The royals' favourite photographer, then as now, was Arthur Edwards of The Sun.

And I too was occasionally carried away by it all. On the occasion of a royal visit to San Diego I was persuaded by NBC News to explain the mystique of the monarchy while wearing a baseball hat inscribed with the words 'Welcome Liz and Phil'.

What we were trying to do, as innovators in the 1980s, was to break out from the old regime of subservient press coverage delivered in boiler-plate prose. We were after all supposed to be journalists not courtiers. The scripts back then were like plates of words bolted together in a shed. 'Princess Margaret arrived at Blackpool Airport to be met by the Earl of Derby the Lord Lieutenant' (film of handshake). 'She looked radiant in an elegant lime green ensemble' (film of smile, dress, and hat). 'She planted a tree in the grounds of the St Mary Hospice' (film of tree). 'Then she mixed and mingled with the staff' (film of staff) 'before leaving for the next routine and boring engagement' (I made up that bit). The adjective of choice was 'radiant', to be applied only to the ladies of the family.

Prince Philip and the reptiles

The Duke of Edinburgh, being notoriously grumpy, could never be described as radiant. The reptiles were ambivalent about him, for he invariably made newsworthy waves. At the Commonwealth Heads of

Government Conference in Cyprus in 1993 a well-known TV reporter was challenged by a colleague to introduce the phrase 'Phil the Greek' into one of his scripts. 'The arrival of the Queen and the Duke,' he wrote, 'will fill the Greeks with pride'. He won the bet.

Royal tours would often start with a reception for the press on board the Royal Yacht, until it was retired in 1997. At one of these the Queen's press secretary introduced a reporter assigned to cover it. "Your Majesty, this is Keith Graves of the BBC." "Oh," she said, "I mostly watch ITN myself." To which Keith replied, "I didn't come here to be insulted."

Tame reptiles find their voices

Back in the 1960s, to my reptilian mind, the media were absurdly obsequious to the monarchy. The news agencies, the Press Association, and Extel, had court correspondents who wore top hats and morning dress and operated out of Buckingham Palace as its unfiltered spokesmen. We called them Tweedledum and Tweedledee. The broadcast reports in the early delays of TV news were delivered in the hushed and reverential tones of a Golden-Microphone-in-Waiting.

That was bound to change, and it did. The principal agent of change was Anthony Carthew, ITN's royal correspondent in the 1970s and 1980s, who pioneered a style that was irreverent without being impudent: part travelogue, part parody, part fashion note, and part political commentary. The BBC's coverage when I started was watched closely in two palaces, Buckingham and Alexandra (then the home of TV news), and laboured beneath the weight of the solemnity expected of it. Under Carthew's influence we managed to lighten it up. But yet it required more crafting than, say, political reporting or war reporting. And it still does.

This reptile becomes an MP

In my next career as a Member of Parliament, the relationship with royalty was completely different. Diana was by then divorced and the ex officio leader of the campaign to eliminate landmines. I spoke up for her in the House of Commons when she was accused of trespassing into politics. She invited me to Kensington Palace, where she referred to her critics as 'those dreadful Tories'.

Then the Queen invited a group of backbenchers to a reception at Buckingham Palace. She told me that she and the Duke had placed bets on the result of the Tatton election in 1997. He had backed the frontrunner, a certain Neil Hamilton. She backed the outsider, me.

The monarchy's and the reptiles' futures

In the years ahead the monarchy of King Charles III will face a resurgent campaign by republicans who wish to abolish it. They are a vociferous minority whose slogan is 'Not My King'. At least a thousand of them demonstrated in Trafalgar Square at the time of his coronation. They were marginalised by the police who arrested their leaders and by the TV producers who largely ignored them. But they will not be silenced.

It is my personal view, as a seasoned ex-reptile, that the broadcasters especially should give them a fair hearing. The monarchy will survive because it is more attractive than the alternative. It protects the role of Head of State from the factionalism of party politics. It would be a national tragedy if our proud army regiments were obliged to swear their allegiance to an elected political grifter; if the Royal Mail were to become the Republican Mail; if the Royal Courts of Justice were to renamed the People's Courts; and if the Royal Society for the Protection of Birds were to transpose its initials and become the SPRB, the Society for the Protection of Republican Birds. We can do better than that. We are in large measure who we were – and the monarchy is central to who we were, and now to who we are.

It is not as if we had never experienced the alternative. We were a republic once – a Commonwealth under a Lord Protector – in the seventeenth century. It was not a happy interlude, especially for the King, and the monarchy was restored by popular acclaim. It has been with us ever since in prosperity and adversity. But it will not survive in this century unaided and on its own. We will do well to support it, loyally and steadfastly, long to reign over us.

About the contributor

Martin Bell was a BBC correspondent for 35 years. He served principally as a war reporter, beginning in Vietnam and ending in Bosnia. He was wounded by mortar fire in Sarajevo in 1992. He was also a royal reporter from time to time. In 1997 he became the Member of Parliament for Tatton, the first elected Independent since 1951. Since 2001 he has been a Goodwill Ambassador for UNICEF UK. He is the author of nine books about soldiering, war, and politics.

Chapter 5

Royal reporting: From deference to disgrace, and death in Paris

Veteran British court correspondent **Michael Cole** asks how it all went wrong for the British royal family, how they lost their mystique, and gained their celebrity

Clement Attlee stepped out of No.10 Downing Street and paused on the doorstep. A BBC man approached diffidently holding a microphone the size of a soup plate.
"Have you anything to say, Prime Minister?"
"No," said Attlee, "I have nothing to say."
"Thank you, Prime Minister."
With that, Mr Attlee gave a wintry smile and got in his car, satisfied that his duty to the Fourth Estate had been fulfilled.

Deference was built into British society until comparatively recently. To my mother and most ordinary people in Britain after World War Two, the medallists in the Respect Olympics were: the Holy Trinity (Gold), the Royal Family (Silver), and the Prime Minister of the Day (Bronze), preferably Winston Churchill but others were acceptable.

Royalty were big beneficiaries of this. No one would have dreamed of waving a microphone under a royal nose.

When Lord Altrincham ventured some mild criticisms of the Queen, saying she spoke 'like a prissy schoolgirl', the newspapers in 1957 condemned his outrageous attacks on her dignity, although they were perfectly fair, which she promptly acknowledged by changing her tone.

'Jesus wept'; Dimbleby apologises

As late as 1965, when the great Richard Dimbleby, who reinvented royalty for the television age, inadvertently blasphemed on air, saying 'Jesus wept!', not realising he was live, after repeated technical failures on the live feed of pictures from West Germany during the Queen's historic first state visit. The uproar continued until he dropped a coin in the Swear Box at the start of his next Panorama.

Even 20 years later, in 1985, when I was 'volunteered' to be BBC TV's Court Correspondent, accredited to Buckingham Palace and allowed to park my red BBC Rover 216 in the courtyard, my respect for the royal institution was taken for granted by my bosses; but it would no longer be unconditional respect or I would have declined the job. The story, I insisted, had to come first.

Heseltine rattles the royal cage

Things had already started to change. The ground rules were bending. And it was, in Sun speak, 'The Royals Wot Started It'. Or rather, it was a short, neatly dressed man from Australia with abundant charm and a slight but endearing speech impediment. William Heseltine may have been the son of a train driver but he was a diplomat and courtier to his manicured fingertips.

He was a breath of fresh air at Buckingham Palace after turgid years in which the Queen's Press Secretary had been the Abominable No Man, declining comment on most stories and refusing access of any kind, whenever and wherever possible.

Clever Bill convinced The Firm, CEO the Duke of Edinburgh, to allow up-close and personal filming which in due course would become The Royal Family, a 1969 documentary of staged tableaux with a few precious sequences that were spontaneous and therefore revealing.

Stepping down from their pedestal for a television programme was dangerous. Some precautions were taken. The film was made by the BBC but the Queen insisted upon retaining the copyright. That meant that it has never been shown in its entirety since the original 1969 broadcasts, with only excerpts ever shown and then by special permission.

I say 'broadcasts' because the Queen also insisted that the film be freely available to ITV, which showed it after the BBC. The Queen was adamant that no news organisation should ever have a royal exclusive. If that happened, she knew that it would, firstly, annoy those not granted the exclusive, and, secondly, create aggressive competition for exclusives, as subsequently happened with disastrous results.

Secrets of the Royal Rota

That was also the reasoning behind the Royal Rota. There was nothing mysterious about it but it is now seriously misunderstood by Prince Harry and his wife who both clearly believe the Rota is a means by which Buckingham Palace controls the Press. As if.

No. In my day the Royal Rota was an elegant lady called Lydia Rider who perched in the corner of the reporters' room at BBC Television News, with her cacti and cheese plants. Lydia sent out the Rota passes, on an even-handed basis, to news organisations to make sure everyone had equal access to royal events, with those not accommodated entitled to the copy and images on a pool basis.

This was eminently sensible. It took the pressure off the Palace and news media alike. It all went wrong — and this was the historic parting of the ways — when in 1985 ITN was secretly given exclusive access to Prince Charles and Princess Diana for a year, a whole year!

This deal was cooked up by Alistair Burnett, the hard-drinking former editor of The Daily Express who had become the star newscaster at ITN, over drinks with the Queen Mother at Sandown Park racecourse in 1984. She undertook to persuade her favourite grandson, Prince Charles, to agree to this unprecedented arrangement.

He did and it resulted in two hour-long documentaries, run in tandem: The Prince and Princess of Wales in Public and then, even more enticingly, ...in Private.

ITN made a lot of money from the twin programmes. They were sold internationally from 1985. If this was not the shot that was heard around the world, it was certainly the start of open season on the royal family.

Genie out of the bottle?

They had put themselves in the shop window, to be admired. Now, they were now undeniably a commercial property. Now, everybody wanted some of that. But some of the coverage would not be what they intended. It would be critical and robustly so.

The flattering follow spot on Prince Charming and Cinderella could instantly become the lurid glare that signals the entry of the Ugly Sisters, as Princess Diana and Sarah Ferguson would become, alternating between being In or Out of favour with the newspapers, like weathermen.

The 1987 broadcast of the BBC's It's a Royal Knockout starring Prince Andrew, Sarah Ferguson, Princess Anne, and the putative showbiz titan Prince Edward as its producer contributed to the coming media disaster.

For an institution that had flourished by being discreet — 'Less is more' was not a cliché then but the Queen might have coined it - this departure from its even-handed and slightly aloof relationship with the media was trouble in the making. And it came just as the number of news outlets was increasing. With increased competition, came the growing appetite for personality-led 'news' and celebrity culture.

The royal family had stooped to conquer. Even though there was not a single good reason for doing so, they had cast themselves as celebrities. Inevitably, it all became very ugly.

Princess Diana and her death in Paris

The monstering of Princess Diana was, in my view, disgusting. I heard paparazzi - thugs with cameras - boasting, "I just hit Diana" or "I did Diana". There was something undeniably sexual about the pursuit. And huge sums of money were there to be made.

The French paparazzo who shot 'The Kiss', a long-range photograph purporting to show Diana and her lover Dodi Fayed embracing on the deck of a yacht in the summer of 1997, got £250,000 for his fuzzy image from Tina Weaver, the editor of The Sunday Mirror. And that was by no means the record price for an intrusive snap of royalty off duty or off guard.

And so it continued until, as her brother Earl Spencer said in his funeral eulogy at Westminster Abbey, Diana the huntress of Greek mythology became Diana the Hunted, pursued to her death in the Alma Tunnel in Paris in the early hours of 31 August 1997, the paparazzi motor drives continuing to whir as the Princess, conscious and able to speak, fought for her life in the back seat of the car.

British tabloids discover ethics?

There was a collective sigh of relief in Fleet Street that no British publication had a photographer at the crash scene, though some papers were offered the pictures which, in a late show of compassion and discretion, they didn't publish but did put in the safe.

The shock of the Princess's death initiated a partial clean-up of the British Press. But the phone-hacking scandals were yet to come, only exposed when the News of the World hacked a recorded message left by Tom Bradby of ITN on the phone of the Private Secretary of Prince William and Prince Harry, offering to loan them some expensive ITN equipment for a private video project, fresh evidence of the strange, ambiguous, symbiotic relationship between royalty and reporters.

My phone was hacked by the same team at the now defunct News of the World. They went to jail. Their conduct was disgraceful but it did not shake my belief in the importance of a free press, needed now more than ever.

Were the great 19th century constitutional writer Walter Bagehot around today, he would not be warning against letting light in upon the magic of monarchy. It's too late for that. Rather, Bagehot would be advising that decency, honesty, and plain dealing should shape the relationship between King Charles III and the media because a constitutional monarchy suits the British temperament in many ways. Its demise would be a loss to both sovereign and his subjects.

About the contributor

Michael Cole worked for the BBC from 1968 to 1988. After reporting from 56 countries he then worked as court correspondent accredited to Buckingham Palace. After leaving the BBC he joined the Harrods and House of Fraser Group, had a seat on the main board of the holding company, and was their Director of Public Affairs for ten years. He left Harrods in 1998 to establish his own public relations and broadcasting company, Michael Cole & Company Limited. He now broadcasts on royal and other topics for all British television channels and radio stations, and writes feature articles for most British national newspapers.

Chapter 6

Getting blood out of a royal stone

*In a fifty-year career in journalism **Charles Rae** spent eighteen of those years as royal correspondent for TODAY and The Sun. Here he recalls some of his adventures getting some of those stories*

Royal reporting is unlike other specialist journalistic jobs in newspapers. In practically all other areas you can manage to speak to the principals of a particular government department or most other organisations who can usually easily be approached for quotes. Most politicians make themselves readily available to deliver their words of wisdom to fight their corner. The same can be said for high ranks in the police and the NHS.

'The Firm' off the record

But covering 'the Firm' is completely different. You cannot ring up the monarch or any other senior royal to ask for a few words on any subject, especially controversial topics affecting the family. There is only one exception and that is on overseas tours where the royal in question usually holds a reception for the travelling press. Here you can get amazing insights by talking to royals. But highly sensitive discussions are taboo and are strictly off the record. But the information gathered can be stored away for another time which gives you great material for future projects.

I was lucky enough to meet all the major royals in my years of covering them and enjoyed and cherished those rare few minutes you get. They are special occasions.

My royal journey

I moved from The Sun, where I was Industrial Editor, to TODAY in 1988 and was soon asked to delve into the troubled world of the royal family. It did not take long to work out that I would be facing a block on information from those who served their royal masters. When I returned to The Sun on the closure of TODAY, I continued to cover the royals.

This was a world far removed from my own, born in Glasgow, living in a tenement in Maryhill, and eventually being asked to leave school as teachers felt they could no longer do anything worthwhile with me. For a time at the start of my royal reporting career, I felt I had bitten off more than I could chew.

The old gatekeepers of the palaces: 'No comment'

In those days those who worked in the lavish surroundings of Buckingham and St James Palaces, and whose job it was to deal with the press, regarded journalists as an irritant. I suspect some still do to this day. Press relations were still in the hands of courtiers, and the daily Court Circular was as close as they ever came to issuing a statement. The palace press office is not there to act in the understood public relations sense. Then it was a hive of courtiers who stage-managed royal tours, helped prepare the anodyne royal speeches, and presented the media with the blandest of faces whenever anything really interesting happened.

In fact, I soon came to believe that these backstage mandarins only knew two words of the English language: No Comment. So, it was back to the drawing board, and I had to learn quickly. I soon discovered that only about half a dozen people close to the royal family could point you in the right direction. It was a steep learning curve. Now I knew the game, I was quite happy at lobbing stories into the various press offices and getting the curt 'no comment' reply.

This is why on royal stories you will always see the ubiquitous 'source' always quoted. It does not mean made up; it purely means that you need to grant anonymity to someone who knows what is going on.

How times changed

But things were soon to change when both Palaces suddenly woke up to the fact that they were getting a terrible pasting as the War of the Waleses got under way. The battle between Diana, Princess of Wales, and her husband Prince Charles saw a sea change in the attitude of some of the team who worked in Palace communications. The PR war between Charles and Diana was in full flow and as far as tabloid editors were concerned it was open season.

It was difficult for the press officers to try to stay aloof from the royal brawling between Diana and Charles, as there were so many 'friends' who were prepared to brief reporters, clearly with the blessing of either the Princess or Prince.

Most of what I call the new breed had a track record of working as civil servants in government departments and press offices. None of them was ever going to ring you up and give you a juicy piece of information for your next page lead or splash. That was never their job. It was always my job to find the stories, but now we had a group of people who clearly were prepared to say more than 'no comment'. They realised that it was important that no comment was no longer going to cut it and that the deference once shown by newspapers to the royal family was gone.

They also realised it was necessary to communicate with the dreaded tabloids, read by the vast majority of the country, and not just toss the odd bone to the likes of The Daily Telegraph or The Times.

The good 'uns

This is why people like Allan Percival, Sandy Henny, Colleen Harris at St James Palace, and Ailsa Anderson and Samantha Cohen at Buckingham Palace all had reasonably good relationships with royal correspondents. They were respected and I like to think that respect was mutual. They usually remained nameless and went by the collective name of 'A royal spokesman said'.

For most of them, however, they entered a world for which no amount of civil service training could prepare them. Despite that, they all left their mark on the institution. There was only one rule that existed between both sides: if you lie you will never be trusted again.

Rocky seas meant a new modus operandi

They had a lot of fallouts to deal with during their time at the helm: Diana's Panorama interview, Jonathan Dimbleby's ITV interview with her husband Prince Charles, Diana's tragic death, dealing with the interests of her grieving sons, William and Harry, the problem of rebuilding Camilla's reputation after her affair with the Prince, and a whole host of other controversies.

Following Diana's death in particular, there was a new understanding on both sides of the barricades. Tabloid editors sat on stories and photographs they would have rushed into print in the mid-1990s. Likewise, St James's Palace, through events carefully managed, allowed access that would have been unimaginable prior to the demise of Diana.

The tabloid 633 squadron

An example of the old guard not caring much about journalists came in July 1993 when Princess Diana visited Zimbabwe, where the highlight of her tour was helping to serve at a soup kitchen deep in the bush. Her press officer had organised buses to take us to the venue – a SIX-HOUR JOURNEY from Harare and six hours back again. Too long for UK deadlines. When we pointed out that we needed to be able to file our stories and pictures, his reply was, "I am not a bloody travel agent!" Diana herself was flying in and out.

I managed to hire four planes and take most of us to the venue, the only proviso being that we arrive before her and leave after her. It was worth it to see the face of the PR man as he saw us waiting for the Princess as he stepped off the plane.

We felt like 633 Squadron, almost flying in formation, and landing way before the Princess. The job itself screamed into the papers. How could it fail?

Advising the Queen

I have only sacrificed one royal story and that came in 2002 when the Queen made a Golden Jubilee visit to Northern Ireland.

We arrived in Omagh where the Queen was to make one visit, to a local library, her only engagement in the town. I was stunned that no arrangement had been made for her to pay her respects in recognition of what happened in 1998 when 29 people were killed in the Real IRA bombing.

On the eve of her visit I was in an hotel with some relatives of the victims of the bombing who were getting angrier and angrier at the perceived slight.

It would have been easy for me to leave things as they were and get a great story about the Queen ignoring the Omagh victims. But I decided quietly to call Ailsa Anderson, Buckingham Palace's Director of Communications, and warn her that the Queen would receive massive criticism that an opportunity to show solidarity with the victims of Omagh was about to be missed. I suggested that she contact then Northern Ireland secretary Dr. John Reid, who ironically had gone to the same school as me, to put him in the picture.

The result was officials on the tour realised how bad things could be and quickly fitted in a visit to the bomb site. The Queen spent several minutes listening to Dr Reid's description of the horror, looking up at buildings on both sides of Market Street. One side of the street has been rebuilt, while construction work continued on the other.

Witness to the royal soap opera

I have always regarded the royal family as one huge real-life soap where many scriptwriters would find some of the plots too outrageous even for television. But it is a fascinating subject, and it is the gift that keeps on giving to journalists. Its machinations are one of the cornerstones of news, whether in print or broadcast.

Would I have changed anything – NO! I enjoyed the chase and I hope the current crop of royal correspondents have as much fun as I did.

About the contributor

Charles Rae has been a journalist for over fifty years, working at The Daily Star, TODAY, and The Sun. He held many specialist roles, including royal correspondent, industrial editor, and consumer editor. He has published three books: Diana: The People's Princess — A Tribute In Words and Pictures (1997); The Queen Mum — Her First Hundred Years (2000), and Fleet Street Frolics! Read All About It (2013). He now commentates on royal matters for many organisations including talkRadio, GB News, LBC, and BBC 3 Counties Radio.

Chapter 7

Reporting royalty: Janus journalism

The Daily Telegraph columnist **Robin Aitken** *argues that the media is too careful with the royal family. A truly conservative position is different*

My own involvement with royal reporting makes for a very short and inglorious story. I was once a reporter for BBC 1's Breakfast News where I covered many stories but I always avoided reporting on royal matters; it didn't interest me and there were many others eager to do it. My luck changed in the fateful late summer of 1997 with the death of Diana, Princess of Wales in a Paris car crash.

Di mania

It was a Sunday morning and, very early, I got a tense phone call from some senior editorial figure and was ordered to turn up later in the day to do my bit. My assignment turned out to be watching the arrival of the Princess' body at Northolt aerodrome in West London. By then it was clear something had gripped the public imagination in an astonishing way; even with the news barely twelve hours old people had begun to line the streets in collective displays of grief. It was a news story for the ages: the nation (and it seemed the rest of the world) was plunged into ostentatious grief for the world's most glamorous woman.

But Breakfast News and the BBC generally alighted on a particular narrative: Diana as a tragic figure, the public's emotional response as authentic and laudable, the rest of the royal family, including the Queen, as cold-hearted formalists. The TV image that stays with me from that time is of some reporter, surrounded by mounds of flowers, vox popping bystanders about their feelings. It seemed to me a kind of performative grief. Most coverage was cloyingly empathetic and – to some of us – emetic. It wasn't for me and much to my relief I was switched to work on a long-term project which would be needed when the fuss died down. As it happens, that took many months.

There was a small irony in this because I have always been a convinced royalist — unlike, it should be said, many of my BBC colleagues. There are no statistics on the matter (very wisely the BBC understands that the last thing it needs is for there to be any accurate survey of the political attitudes of BBC staff) but my informed guess is that republican sentiment is much stronger in the Corporation than in the general public. The BBC's conscience is non-conformist, the spirit of the Levellers lives on in its ranks, it is anti-aristocratic.

Should conservatives support the monarchy?

The philosopher Roger Scruton said that to be a conservative is to cherish the good things handed down to us by previous generations. It is therefore axiomatic that true conservatives are, in the British context, monarchists. That seems obvious to me but what should the true conservative attitude be to the royal family itself? To support the idea of monarchy in argument and debate goes without saying; but conservatives are not obliged to admire or be interested the royal family per se. The utility of monarchy is the thing which conservatives should value, not its potential to fill gossip columns.

The strongest conservative arguments in support of monarchy are founded in utility, even though the institution itself depends upon popular sentiment, not constitutional logic, for its survival. A constitutional monarchy brings continuity and stability and operates according to the timescale dictated by human mortality, not politics. We live in an era of meritocracy so the existence of an institution centred on a family which owes its position to heredity, not merit, might seem anomalous, and is, to some people, offensively anachronistic. But, counter-intuitively, it is exactly because the House of Windsor is a pillar of an aristocratic system founded on bloodlines, that it is so valuable because – this is the crucial point – the throne is beyond ambition. No thrusting democrat, beating her way through the thickets of British political life, can ever set her sights on the throne; it is a role set-apart and denuded, insofar as that is possible, of political partisanship. We are thus spared the often divisive contests which republics have to endure.

At best republics end up with presidents who are grey figures relegated to ceremonial functions and relative obscurity. (Name the last five Presidents of Germany anybody?). At worst they are powerful chief executives, elected dictators, able to wield great power, not always wisely. Monarchy does not inoculate a country from folly (look at our disastrous entanglement in the Iraq war) but it creates a space at the pinnacle of national life which is outside politics. Happy and sane countries have a limited appetite for politics and I judge there is no great demand for more political combat in the UK.

There always has been a minority opposed to monarchy; in recent years support for abolition fluctuates from the mid-teens to around 30 per cent. To many on the Left this is both a profound disappointment and also something of a puzzle; why do 'the people' put-up with a system which entrenches inequality and is a manifestation of hereditary unfairness? A Marxist might answer 'false consciousness' but a better explanation lies in the human dimension. Each generation of Britons marches in lockstep with each new generation of the Windsors. This synchronisation makes it easy for the ordinary citizen to identify with and project their own feelings on to someone of roughly the same age; in this way a royal family humanises the state. The overwhelming response to Diana's death showed how millions had incorporated her into their interior lives. Diana — and the late Queen Elizabeth II — were much-loved figures in a way no politician ever was.

Diana's TV life after death

Nothing endures for ever, neither kingdoms nor empires nor republics, but for the time being Britain's monarchy looks secure and the media plays a role in this. It is often supportive but its fascination with the royal family sometimes drives it to excess. The limitless appetite for paparazzi pictures of Diana was obsessive and destructive - and then came the interview that Princess Diana gave to Martin Bashir for an edition of BBC's Panorama in 1995. That interview, in which she bared her soul and allowed the nation to share her unhappiness, was a scoop for the ages. It ended her marriage and set her, definitively, outside the royal family. So pleased was the BBC hierarchy with the interview that on the tenth anniversary of its first screening they commissioned a special programme commemorating the event. Many of the BBC's top brass were featured bragging about the cloak-and-dagger techniques they had employed to get the interview and then to keep all knowledge of it a closely guarded secret.

But on the twenty-fifth anniversary of that interview ITV aired a programme about how the Panorama scoop had been obtained. The programme exposed subterfuge and dishonesty completely at odds with the BBC's professedly high-minded journalistic ethics. The BBC commissioned an inquiry which concluded that Bashir had used 'deceitful methods' to obtain the interview. The inquiry laid the blame mostly at Bashir's door, though many very senior BBC reputations were tarnished. The Corporation ended up apologising profusely for its underhandedness and paying damages to an individual scapegoated for institutional failures; Bashir's triumph, it turned out, was the BBC's shame and in New Broadcasting House it was a time of sackcloth and ashes.

Since the Bashir affair the BBC has been conspicuously, one might almost say unctuously, loyal in its royal coverage; perhaps in subconscious expiation for its sins. Royal jubilees, births, marriages, and deaths have all been afforded lavish coverage and the Corporation's critics have been vigilant for any tell-tale signs of disrespect. Meanwhile the rest of the media faithfully follow their established traditions; The Daily Telegraph is loyalist, The Times likewise (though Rupert Murdoch, its proprietor, is a convinced republican); The Daily Mail, The Daily Express, and The Daily Mirror gorge on royal stories indiscriminately and whilst these papers can be critical (Prince Andrew has become a perennial whipping-boy) there is little doubt that they march to a monarchist heartbeat. It is usually left to The Guardian and The Independent to enter a dissenting note but even they, on the really big occasions like the death of the Queen, go big on royal reportage. Among the broadcasters Channel 4, the perpetual adolescent of British broadcasting, often mounts 'cheeky' programmes mocking the royals to satisfy, I assume, forever disappointed chattering-class republicans.

The media and the monarchy are locked in an eternal embrace, but critical coverage notwithstanding, it is the media's fascination with the institution which keeps the show on the road. One purpose of monarchy is to be splendid; people enjoy public spectacle and colourful celebration. For the majority of people monarchy is a freely available and benevolent distraction; they can enjoy it (or, if they choose, ignore it) at no personal cost. The media, in all its forms — fawning or critical, informed or ignorant — plays its part keeping royalty centre stage .

Royalty and media's relationship

The media is Janus-faced about monarchy: often sycophantic, it can turn nasty when it wants, but conservatives should not worry unduly on that score. The occasional spasms of republicanism which grip individual outlets are to be expected. More generalised criticism — as in the wake of Diana's death — will also sometimes happen because the royals are not perfect individuals and even their imperfections are a kind of strength ('they're just like us!'). Furthermore, envy of privilege is natural, healthy even, in a democracy and resentment of their wealth is the price the royal family must bear in return for their gilded lifestyles. But for all the objective absurdity of our system (if we didn't have a legitimate monarch no sensible person, even a committed royalist like me, would consider inventing one) the country, and its media, have reached a happy accommodation with royalty. And we are not alone: there are twelve other monarchies in Europe alone, proof I would argue of the enduring value of constitutional monarchy. In all these countries the royals confer stability and continuity in a public space free of party politics all the while providing endless fodder for journalists. That's not a bad bargain all round.

About the contributor

Robin Aitken is a former BBC news correspondent on Today, The World Tonight, and Breakfast News. He now writes columns for The Daily Telegraph mainly on media matters.

Chapter 8

The missing years: Prince Andrew, celebrity, and the media

Jason Lee addresses a neglected part of media discourse surrounding Prince Andrew, the earlier years of allegations about him (2015 to 2019), and how they relate to the wider allegations of celebrity child sexual abuse and police collusion of this era

Before Prince Andrew's 2019 Newsnight interview, he was known as the former playboy prince 'Randy Andy', but most people would not have associated him with child abuse. This is despite it being public knowledge that Prince Andrew had known financier Jeffrey Epstein since 1999, and Virginia Giuffre alleging in 2014 that she had been sex trafficked by Epstein to Prince Andrew. Analysis of news articles between 2015 to 2019 suggest little occurred on this front from a royal perspective. What stunned audiences in 2019 was the TV defence of his relationship with convicted paedophile Epstein. Just six per cent of Britons believed Prince Andrew's account of his friendship with Epstein (Smith 2019).

Contrary to popular opinion, the media was soft in reporting on Prince Andrew's known dubious relationships. Stories were killed off between 2015 to 2019. As we shall see, it was reported that members of Prince Andrew's security detail were paid to turn a blind eye to Prince Andrew's activities connected to Epstein. This was all in the public domain four years prior to the Newsnight interview. Due to strong libel laws and an informal agreement between the media and Buckingham Palace, Prince Andrew's involvement with the child sex trafficking couple Ghislaine Maxwell (daughter of the former Mirror owner Robert Maxwell) and Epstein remained mostly unreported. Fictionalised accounts did exist (Lee 2014).

The vocalising of child abuse narratives in the 1980s arose during a period when other unifying narratives were collapsing, serving a social purpose, sociologically termed a metanarrative (Jenks 2016). This was true in the 1980s and 1990s (Lee 2005) but by 2015, with adherence to traditional religious belief systems in the ascendant, this needed questioning. In January 2015 the UK media highlighted Prince Andrew's role in a paedophile case in Florida, but it took another four years before he made his public defence of his behaviour on Newsnight.

Politics, media, and celebrity: an easy smokescreen

Paedophile conspiracies abounded in this period. One concerned presenter Jill Dando who was fatally shot in Fulham in 1999. Within conspiracy paradigms, she knew about wider sexual abuse conspiracies. These theories bled into the mainstream press (Hale 2014). Celebrity stories like these swamped any royal ones. Dando was a close friend of singer Sir Cliff Richard who in 2014 was accused, but never charged, with paedophilia. The media, in collaboration with the police, created a spectacle where the viewer could watch as police broke into Richard's apartment seeking evidence.

Heavily criticised for not doing anything over paedophile TV star Jimmy Savile, the BBC wanted to be seen as leading on a mediated child protection event, but this backfired. UK police were being asked to reduce budgets by over 20 per cent, so the police focusing on an accusation from 40 years ago was questioned. Through spectacle, the media reinforces the idea that the police are working to protect the nation. Here was an ageing accused pop star who has permanently left the UK, just prior to another ageing star, Gary Glitter, returning to face charges of child sexual abuse in 2015. According to substantiated evidence, Jimmy Savile was a mentor to Prince Charles (Davies 2015). The useful working-class elite was seemingly protected by the upper class and vice versa.

See no evil, hear no evil

As noted, in terms of police protection, Prince Andrew had two publicly funded bodyguards. In tabloid reports of 2015, quoting bodyguard sources, these guards turned a blind eye to his activities at Jeffrey Epstein's properties (Wright and Greenhill 2015). The aftermath of the 2021 kidnap and rape of Sarah Everard by Metropolitan Police protection officer Wayne Couzens verifies that a culture of misogyny existed, especially in the elite protection services. Paid twice as much as normal officers, given the overtime, it makes sense they would do as they were told for financial benefits. From the culture we see how people were enabled, personal gain placed first.

Jim Fixed It

Allegations abounded about Jimmy Savile early on, but evidence passed to the police was 'lost'. How Savile managed to avoid prosecution is difficult to say, but his connection to powerful politicians and royalty, including the now King Charles, are well-known. He ran a private club for police officers. In 2013 the Independent Police Complaints Commission (IPCC) launched an investigation into Mick Starkey of West Yorkshire Police, allegedly a member of Savile's Friday Morning Club, attended by serving and retired officers. Connections between Savile and the police were not hidden, his financial donations to charities linked to West Yorkshire Police well-known. His club is thought to have run for at least twenty years (Schute 2016). The Metropolitan Police, the largest in the UK, and continually thought to be corrupt, as evidenced again by the Casey Review published in March 2023, decided to not investigate allegations against Prince Andrew. This is part of a similar pattern of avoiding facing this issue exacerbating further corruption (Harper 2022).

Blind eyes or collusion?

Police collusion with paedophiles is different to turning a blind eye which was one accusation from the former girlfriend of rock group Lost Prophets front man Ian Watkins. The IPCC investigated why the police ignored warnings, given that Watkins was reported to the police four times in four years before he was arrested. Eight officers were investigated, the IPCC concerned that it was his celebrity status that slowed the process. This does have overlaps with the Savile and Prince Andrew cases in terms of failed police procedures. On 14 January 2015 Watkins' ex-girlfriend Joanne Mjadzelics was cleared of all charges on child sex abuse image offences. She claimed she was trying to trap Watkins, and had alerted the police in 2008, five years before he was sentenced to 35 years. Parallels with Prince Andrew and Savile are overt: protecting the celebrity rather than children. In the initial police report it was claimed there was no evidence, that they were only allegations made by a disgruntled ex-partner.

Police collusion or cover-up?

As with Prince Andrew, in the Watkins case the authorities' misogyny played its part. The police took the side of the celebrity. The voice of one woman was pitted against one man, plus a group of men – the police. There was the issue of mental health: stories are doubted and people are demonised. Abnormal pathology in many cases is part of celebrity culture, especially erotomania (Redmond 2014: 115). This police corruption was not just limited to the South Wales Police, where officers faced gross misconduct charges, but also Bedfordshire Police, and South Yorkshire Police. As more new stories were released about celebrities, police incompetence was ignored, and reporting on royal connections to cases curtailed.

Publicist Max Clifford is an interesting parallel example, given how close he was to all the main celebrities of the era. Clifford was arrested in December 2012 under Operation Yewtree, set up following the Jimmy Savile revelations. Allegations dated back to 1977. At first, much of the media spun the story in Clifford's favour, claiming girls were looking for a career break. Clifford did not denounce girls as gold-diggers, as did Savile and Andrew's legal team. He was found guilty of eight counts of indecent assault on girls as young as 14, receiving eight years in prison. The media ignored the judge's comment that he was certain Clifford had assaulted a 12-year-old girl.

So, from 2015 to 2019 the media mainly ignored royal stories linked to child sexual abuse focusing on politicians and celebrities as briefly explained here. Academic presses were also uninterested in Prince Andrew's case from fear of being sued (Lee 2018). Only when Prince Andrew decided to do an interview, erroneously attempting to kill the story, did media discourse surrounding child sexual abuse in a royal context advance.

Still missing years?

Instead of facing a trial, Prince Andrew gathered what is thought to be $16.3 million to pay off Giuffre, never admitting guilt but by paying her off understanding he probably would have been convicted had he gone to trial.

Bill Gates, Bill Clinton, Kevin Spacey, and many others were associates of Epstein. Like Savile, Epstein did charitable work as a smokescreen. Giuffre is thoroughly convincing when she speaks of being raped by Prince Andrew. She was part of the evidence that convicted Epstein, so the court and jury believed her. The media love 'paedo-hunter' stories and while these groups have brought about convictions cases have been damaged through these actions. By law we are all innocent until proven guilty, but it is a fact that royals are seemingly above the law, or change the law to benefit themselves, as Elizabeth II did to protect her wealth.

According to Emily Maitlis, Andrew thought the Newsnight interview had gone well. Reports from a variety of sources, including people who worked for Epstein, of Prince Andrew frolicking in the pool on Epstein's private island with half-naked women, plus guards being paid to ignore his behaviour, exist. But the royal family has been good at quashing stories. Time and again the police have 'lost' or ignored evidence, or perhaps been more culpable.

Prince Harry let it all hang out in his memoir. If we are to believe him from his April 2023 court case, a relationship existed between the Murdoch press and the royals with regards to phone hacking which meant Prince William did not go to court but received a substantial pay-off. There was a quid pro quo involving silence. Epstein's death is suspicious, according to his own brother. He had CCTV on his properties. Some compare the royal family to the British mafia and the arms of 'the firm' are long. Where is the video-footage of Prince Andrew? Maxwell might know, but she is not talking — yet.

References

Dan Davies (2015) In Plain Sight: The Life and Lies of Jimmy Savile, London: Quercus.
Don Hale (2014) 'Tragic Jill Dando probed BBC paedo ring', The Daily Star, 21 July, www.dailystar.co.uk/news/latest-news/389922-Tragic-Jill-Dando-probed-BBC-PAEDO-ring (accessed 25 April 2023).
Tom Harper (2022) Broken Yard: The Fall of the Metropolitan Police, London: Biteback.
Chris Jenks (2016) Childhood, London: Routledge.
Jason Lee (2018) 'Academics Should Not Be So Wary of Researching Royalty', Times Higher Education, 3 December.
Jason Lee (2014) Unholy Days, London: Roman.
Jason Lee (2005) Pervasive Perversion, London: Free Association.
Press Association (2015) 'Ian Watkins ex-lover found not guilty over child abuse images', The Guardian, 14 January, http://www.theguardian.com/uk-news/2015/jan/14/ian-watkins-ex-lover-not-guilty-child-abuse-images-joanne-mjadzelics-lostprophets (accessed 25 April 2023).

Sean Redmond (2014) Celebrity and the Media, London: Palgrave.

Joe Schute (2016) 'How far did police go to protect Jimmy Savile?', The Daily Telegraph, 18 October 2013 www.telegraph.co.uk/news/uknews/crime/jimmy-savile/10389041/How-far-did-police-go-to-protect-Jimmy-Savile.html (accessed 25 April 2023).

Matthew Smith (2019) 'Just 6% of Britons believe Prince Andrew's account of his friendship with Jeffrey Epstein', YouGov, 18 November, Just 6% of Britons believe Prince Andrew's account of his friendship with Jeffrey Epstein | YouGov (accessed 25 April 2023).

Stephen Wright and Sam Greenhill (2015) 'Prince Andrew's guards turned 'blind eye'', Mail Online, 11 January, www.dailymail.co.uk/news/article-2905850/Andrew-s-guards-turned-blind-eye-Yard-officers-watched-Duke-partied-young-girls-says-Epstein-s-butler.html (accessed 25 April 2023).

About the contributor

Jason Lee is Professor of Film, Media, and Culture at De Montfort University. He is a Chartered Psychologist, and a British Academy Innovation Fellow. Lee is the author or editor of twenty books, including several on child sexual abuse and the media. More on Lee, including a BBC interview, can be found at www.cjplee.com

Chapter 9

The princes and the press: nothing new here to see or hear

*The BBC promised its 2021 series The Princes and the Press would examine royal 'briefings and counter-briefings', as well investigating 'whether negative stories about the royals were based on information from people connected to other royal households'. After watching the series, **Michael Cole** found the royal family had little to worry about*

What was all the fuss about? The Princes and the Press, the BBC's November 2021 bombshell two-part documentary series, meant to blow the doors off Kensington Palace with revelations about Harry and William at war, was a damp squib.

After one hour of the 22 November programme what had we learned? Royals prefer positive stories to negative ones; what a surprise. Prince Harry hates the media; who knew? Meghan Markle didn't bully her staff; wow! The Duchess of Sussex had authorised her lawyer, Jenny Afia, to say so. Has anyone, anywhere, ever admitted to being a bully, the most repulsive of failings?

Ms. Afia was one of the few new faces in the first programme that, the BBC had claimed, 'tells the story of one of the most dramatic periods in modern royal history, looking at how the younger royal relationship with the media changed following the Queen's Diamond Jubilee'.

Really? Where was the drama? What were the changes? The series failed to come up with the goods and must go down as the BBC giving the royal edifice a gentle going-over with a feather duster.

The royal right of reply at the end of the programme, with the Queen, Prince Charles, and Prince William combining to train their 16 inch guns on the BBC, complaining that 'too often overblown and unfounded claims from unnamed sources are presented as fact', looked like the overreaction of someone flinching before a blow has landed.

It was written before they saw the programme. They had little to worry about. Eighty hours of interviews had been distilled into a small measure of 50 proof gin, without the bitters.

It was interesting for insiders. I was pleased to see familiar faces explaining how and why they had reported this or that episode in the royal soap opera. So what? It meant little to the ordinary viewer who has enough sense to know that little or nothing has changed, the royal family is fulfilling its destiny, and a free press is doing its job of reporting without fear or favour.

"You cannot report from a kneeling position," is what I told the Editor of BBC TV News when I was 'volunteered' to be its Court Correspondent in 1985. I didn't ask for the job and said I would only do it if I could report royal stories like every other news story, factually, fairly, objectively.

That was agreed, as it had to be. It is the only way to maintain public trust and, to be fair to the royal family, it is the only thing Buckingham Palace ever asked or expected. It is not as if there's ever a need to make anything up. Instances of pure invention are vanishingly rare. A royal reporter has only to look and listen and the stories come thick and fast.

There are no instances of a reporter suggesting to a royal personage that they do something silly or scandalous to get themselves on the front page. As Mr Wemmick says in Great Expectations, by that great reporter Charles Dickens, "They'll do it, if there's anything to be got by it."

The only truly serious matter chronicled by the programme was the criminal hacking carried out by Clive Goodman, the royal editor of the News of the World. But Goodman and Glenn Mulcaire, who did the actual hacking, went to jail in 2006, and the newspaper was closed down in 2011.

As one who was hacked, I was glad to see an end to a disreputable episode in British journalism. But I take comfort that it was revealed by a free press and properly punished. But all this was already well known.

One of the programme's few new and compelling moments was the interview with a chastened and apparently contrite private investigator Gavin Burrows, who had done some of the hacking and surveillance on Prince Harry and his then girlfriend Chelsey Davy, who said: "I was basically part of a group of people who robbed him of his normal teenage years."

The series, many months in production, was presented by the BBC's media editor, Amol Rajan, born in Kolkata, and a graduate of Downing College, Cambridge. Rajan is an avowed republican. He twice made clear that he was not delivering judgement on anything. Why not? Much better had he done so, or presented a show defending his view that the monarchy is 'absurd' and the media a 'propaganda outlet'.

The truth is the monarchy suits the British temperament and relies on the press, TV, and radio to maintain its relationship with the people. The time for the monarchy to worry would be when the media were no longer interested. That would mean the show was over.

About the contributor

Michael Cole worked for the BBC from 1968 to 1988. After reporting from 56 countries he then worked as court correspondent accredited to Buckingham Palace. After leaving the BBC he joined the Harrods and House of Fraser Group, had a seat on the main board of the holding company, and was their Director of Public Affairs for ten years. He left Harrods in 1998 to establish his own public relations and broadcasting company, Michael Cole & Company Limited. He now broadcasts on royal and other topics for all British television channels and radio stations, and writes feature articles for most British national newspapers.

SECTION TWO
Courts and coronations

Introduction
Andrew Beck

That was then; this is now. Having examined some of the historical background of British royalty's relations with the media it's now time to shift the focus to that relationship in 2023. In all bar one chapter contributors in Section Two analyse the royal media events of March, April, and May 2023, with especial focus on the weekend of 6/7 May.

Spectacular royal events such as Charles III's coronation bring out the best and the worst in media coverage, and this ceremony and the next day's concert, were no exceptions. In terms of the best we need go no further than the opening of John Mair's evaluation of the coronation as a television event: 'Just marvel at the sheer size of the UK broadcasting operations for the event'. He tracks the way the royal event was clearly made for television, right from the opening shots of Buckingham Palace to the military parade involving nearly 4,000 members of the UK's armed forces. His takeaway from the event: 'The military show-off made the television day'.

In terms of the worst, well there was a lot to choose from, not the least being the farcical heights attained by some commentators' prose, desperately scratching around for something, anything to say about the most minor aspect of the weekend's events. Writing in the 6 May Guardian about Robert Tombs' article 'The mystical power of the spoon' in the same day's edition of The Spectator Marina Hyde came across one such example, and, try as she might, she couldn't stop herself collapsing in hysterics: 'the spoon used to anoint the sovereign with holy oil, which was described as a "very special one" (agreed), "one of the most beautiful examples of that humble genus" (OK), and "doubtless the world's most important spoon" (sorry, I've gone)'.

In spring 2023 as well as the coronation there were other developing events in the British royal soap opera, not least of which was Prince Harry's continuing battle with British tabloid newspapers. Never one to underestimate the impact of a personal appearance he surprised many royal watchers by turning up in the High Court where he accused the Mail and the Sun of illegal breaches of privacy. Former Times executive Liz Gerard writes a fortnightly column for InPublishing where she analyses newspaper coverage of specific topics. In 'Harry goes to court' she presents a mammoth piece of forensic media analysis of Harry's (and other's) legal actions. Putting under the microscope British newspapers' reporting of their own less than decent, legal, and honest behaviour over a 44-day period she tries, almost in vain, to find any national newspaper which 'had presented to its readers a full and fair account of any of the proceedings in the High Court'. Sadly she concludes that while the Times and Telegraph came close 'the rest were either partisan, deliberately blind, or uninterested'.

Sticking with Price Harry and sticking with the courts, in 'A sick relationship' Julian Petley, emeritus professor at Brunel University, offers a very close reading of Spare, Prince Harry's 2023 memoir, and of his witness statements for the High Court. Petley focuses on what emerged from Spare and from various court appearances about the relationship between the British royal family and British media, something of a devil's bargain. The royal family, 'the Institution' in Harry's words, is 'prepared to suffer the worst that the press can throw at them, partly to avoid feeding the beast but also to not jeopardise the more positive coverage that they can engineer'. A veritably Faustian pact.

There has been much media surprise about a living member of the British royal family not only taking legal action in the British courts but also making a personal appearance. Such events, so the shocked reaction went, were unprecedented. Just as during the Covid pandemic when 'unprecedented' was not only the media and political cliché of the day, so too have Harry's court appearances been characterised as 'shocking' or, well, 'unprecedented'. In Section One of this book our contributors examined ways in which the British royal family have, over the years, managed, not to say manipulated, the media. In 'Don't mess with John Wayne or the royals: The media, the law, and the royal family' Coventry University's Law School's Steve Foster takes the historical long view of this relationship and demonstrates that the courts and royalty are no strangers. Covering legal action by Queen Victoria's husband Prince Albert, Princess Diana, the then Duchess of Cambridge, the Sussexes (natch), and even Harry's dad when he was still the Prince of Wales, Foster shows how successful the British royal family has been. As he observes, 'the fact is that when the media have faced legal action from members of the royal family, it has, with rare exceptions, ended up on the losing side, with many decisions safeguarding the privacy and other rights of the royal family also setting wider precedents in this area'.

As any number of observers pointed out both at the time of her death and subsequently, Elizabeth II was much mourned. Clearly she would be a hard act to follow. After his 74 years waiting in the wings for his cue to stride on to the stage as king, Charles III clearly understood this. Sensing how low was his own popularity in comparison with his late mother he might have reflected how one of the features of her time on the throne deemed most successful by politicians, public, and press alike were her international tours. So after becoming king in September 2022 he determined to emulate his late mother as soon as was practicable. While no stranger to royal tours this would be his first as king in his own right rather than as heir in waiting. Initial plans were for Charles to visit France from 26 to 29 March, but President Macron's proposals to raise retirement age to 64 had led to widespread riots in the streets of Paris and other French cities, so his visit was switched from France to Germany. In 'Constructing royal soft power: A tabloid tradition' Loughborough University's Dr Nathan Ritchie offers an incisive analysis of not only this state visit to Germany but also of previous royal tours. The success or otherwise of such state visits is determined by strategic planning by Buckingham Palace and the press, particularly the tabloid press, guided by an age-old formula: (1) the monarch is welcomed by the country they are visiting, 'evidenced by the presence of statesmen and cheering crowds'; (2) they charm 'elite figures and "everyday people" through unique displays of diplomatic skill and appearance'; (3) goodwill is felt by monarch and hosts alike; and (4) afterwards there is a 'sense of lasting national unity between the two countries as a result of the monarch's efforts'. Repeat ad infinitum.

John Mair is an old TV hand. He worked on popular BBC programme formats such as Question Time, he's been a BBC current affairs producer, has made TV documentaries, has worked for ITV and Channel 4, has directed live TV, working on large-scale live programmes such as BBC coverage of UK General Election nights, and watches television with a keen, professional, and seasoned eye. On 6 May 2023 he installed himself on his sofa and watched all British broadcast television coverage of Charles III's coronation. All day. So you didn't have to.

Peter York has worn many hats: among them columnist, author (The Official Sloane Ranger Handbook; Style Wars; Modern Times; Cooler, Faster, More Expensive; The War Against the BBC), television series presenter, co-founder of the SRU management consultancy, and president of the Media Society. In 'Charles III's coronation, a stylists guide' he brings his sharp eye and equally sharp pen to the visual look of that day's events: did it convince as style? He found that the 2023 coronation was no 1953 coronation redux. Stylistically he found the 2023 event all over the place. In 1953 'Lords wore their robes, some of them very old, and peeresses wore tiaras […] And in the endless procession of Ancient Britain proceeding up the aisle there were yet more toffs, or rather super-toffs, like the Duke of Norfolk, who had a definable ceremonial role in the whole affair'. In 2023, in their wish to appear inclusive, the royal family 'absolutely ditched the toffs' and 'the whole ancient notion of Lords spiritual and temporal, in favour of a curious combination of styles and looks'. This leads York to question what is the 'royal family's relationship with what remains of the aristocracy and the assimilated and aspirant plutocracy' and finds it 'deeply conflicted'. Most certainly not a good look for royalty.

GB News is owned by All Perspectives, a holding company. When this new channel was launched in June 2021 its then chairman, Andrew Neil, asserted that it would plug a gap in the television market for 'the vast number of British people who feel underserved and unheard by their media'. Quite possibly taking his cue from the company's name he said the channel would 'champion robust, balanced debate and a range of perspectives on the issues that affect everyone in the UK, and not just those living in the London area'. So far so democratic and non-metropolitan. In 'All perspectives?' I offer a reading of GB News output not only on the day of Charles III's coronation but also in the weeks preceding it. Has it settled down to become a fixture in the British television landscape? Does it represent all perspectives? Is it making the waves and being as disruptive as it hoped to be?

Veteran British journalist (nearly 50 years) and now associate professor of international journalism at Guangdong University of Foreign Studies, Alan Geere undertook a huge task with the coronation weekend's newspapers. Taking himself off to the newsagents and returning home with all of them he set about analysing and evaluating them. In 'What the coronation papers say' he conceived of those newspapers still vying for readers' attention (and hard-earned cash) as a large scale football game. Starting with the pre-match build up, he then moves on to the match itself, and decides which papers were the winners and which papers were the losers.

The novelist William S Burroughs lived in central London, in Mayfair, from 1966 to 1974. Whilst living there he clearly formed an intense dislike of not only the British royal family but also of the way British people venerated them. This clearly rankled with him years after returning to the US: in his 1983 novel The Place of Dead Roads he has his character Kim despair of the UK: 'What hope for a country where people will camp out for three days to glimpse the Royal Couple?' (Burroughs 1983: 194). Although now based in New York Angela Antetomaso spent more than twenty years living and working in London and clearly had a vastly different experience and appreciation of London, the Queen, and all the associated regal pageantry: 'Buckingham Palace, the summer parties, and the Changing of the Guard'. In 'Over there looking at over here (wistfully?)' she offers a detailed account of and a very personal reflection on the experience of watching Charles III's coronation from the other side of the Atlantic Ocean. This in turn prompts her to think further about the 'special relationship', the experience of not living in a monarchy, the striking differences between how Prince Harry is reported at home and abroad, and to closely examine the sometimes lonely, sometimes lost figure Harry cut at his father's coronation. She found herself 'quite taken aback by the disrespect and the outpouring of hostility toward' him. She concludes, 'God save the King. And possibly his broken, divided family'.

Raymond Snoddy has spent nearly 50 years reporting on media issues for The Times, Financial Times, and Independent, presenting BBC's Newswatch, and appearing on BBC, Channel 4, and Sky News commenting on the news industry. Who better, then, to cast his eye over a range of international newspapers to examine how they reported Charles' coronation? In 'Do they mean us? International reaction to the Charles III's coronation' he presents a whirlwind tour of global news media reports about the event. Starting with London newspapers he then heads out to take in US television and newspapers. From there he moves to examine how the event was reported in Australia, New Zealand, France, Germany, Spain, Sri Lanka, Kenya, Uganda, Russia, and Vanuatu. He concludes 'the interest from much of the rest of the world for a coronation in the UK is remarkable by any standards'.

Read on.

References

William S Burroughs (1983) The Place of Dead Roads, New York: Holt, Rinehart, & Winston.
Marina Hyde (2023) 'Hail King Charles: a monarch in his pomp but out of his time', The Guardian, 6 May.

Chapter 10

Harry goes to court

Just how did the UK national press report the Duke of Sussex and his war against the tabloids in April and May 2023?
Liz Gerard takes a long, hard look

In the 45 days from 28 March to 12 May 2023, members of the royal family featured on our national newspaper front pages 320 times. These appearances included 133 photographs and 82 lead stories.

What do you expect? you might ask. We've just had a coronation for the first time in 70 years. And we can all pledge allegiance to the new King. And Kate had a go at climbing a wall. And Charlotte had a birthday. And Louis wore blue. And some of them went to the pub and drank beer or a gin and tonic. And Camilla's a jolly good egg. And Meghan is self-centred. And Harry...

Ah yes, Harry

Harry flew in from America twice during that period. Once to make a brief appearance at the coronation, once to attend the High Court, where he has launched three cases, accusing the Mail, the Sun, and the Mirror of illegal breaches of privacy.

Harry was joined in his case against the Mail by Baroness Lawrence, Elton John, David Furnish, Sadie Frost, Liz Hurley, and Simon Hughes. Only Hurley and Hughes were missing from court on day one – 27 March. Quite a big deal, you might have thought. Five very big names, including a royal prince, appearing in court in person to sue our most popular news brand. Imagine the sort of coverage that turnout would have achieved were they taking on the BBC, rather than the Mail.

So how many of those 320 front-page items did this four-day hearing account for? Six, almost all on the first day. The Times and Telegraph both had a main photograph of Harry with a caption explaining why he was in the country; the i and Mirror had puffs, the i referring to the court case, the Mirror ignoring that altogether in favour of the King being too busy to see his son. The Guardian also had Harry as the main picture, alongside a splash that focused on Doreen Lawrence's assertion that she felt betrayed by the Mail – which has made great capital over the years from its pursuit of her son's murderers.

Harry vs The Mail

But the case was covered inside, wasn't it? Up to a point, Lord Copper. The Times, i and, Telegraph had page leads, the first two focused on the allegations against the Mail; the Telegraph – in common with the other papers that carried anything at all – on the line that Harry wouldn't be seeing dad while he was here. The Mail, which had described the lawsuits as 'a pre-planned and orchestrated attempt to draw it into the phone-hacking scandal' and the allegations as 'preposterous smears', ploughed its own furrow with a page 5 lead headlined 'Key witness says hacking claims 'false''. A private investigator who had told the plaintiffs' lawyers 18 months earlier that he had acted illegally on behalf of the Mail — 'hacking phones, tapping landlines and bugging cars' — had now produced another signed statement retracting it all.

The paper's owner, Associated, wanted the case thrown out, arguing, among other things, that it was based on material given in confidence to the Leveson inquiry and because it was out of time. It also applied for anonymity for its journalists 'in order to prevent distinguished journalists having their reputations destroyed in the event that the case never proceeds to full trial'. The granting of this application was phrased as 'the judge quickly awarded victory to the Mail'. Somehow the factoid that it had been made under the auspices of human rights legislation — which the Mail has repeatedly said should be repealed — did not make it into print.

So much for day one. If Doreen Lawrence was a tasty starter, day two brought a seriously meaty main course in the form of Prince Harry's witness statement. There were two central features:

- The royal family had known about phone hacking, he said, but didn't tell him and did nothing about it for fear of opening a can of worms. There was even, he said, a private agreement with the Murdoch papers not to 'engage or even discuss' the possibility of bringing claims against them until the hacking litigation was over.
- His assertion that he had decided to sue Associated because 'if the most influential newspaper company can evade justice […] the

whole country is doomed'. The statement continued, 'I am bringing this claim because I love my country and I remain deeply concerned by the unchecked power, influence and criminality of Associated. The evidence I have seen shows that Associated's journalists are criminals with journalistic powers which should concern every single one of us. The British public deserve to know the full extent of this cover-up and I feel it is my duty to expose it.'

Wow! Just a reminder, this is a statement by a royal prince in documents to the High Court, not a barb thrown out by some bloke in the pub. And he was there, in the flesh, to hear his words read out. It may be that it shows, as the Mail attests, that he is obsessed. But it surely merits reporting. Apparently not on page 1.

How the street of shame saw it

Only one title — the i — had any mention of the case or Harry's allegations on the cover, and that as a small puff. The Times had a new portrait of the King, the Telegraph told readers that Charles would be dining with his cousins in Germany. Even the Guardian was too busy with its mea culpa on its founder's links to slavery.

Most papers ran page leads inside, although the i and the Times did not mention the alleged pact with its stablemates at News Group Newspapers (the Sun and News of the World's parent company) or Harry's explanation of why he was suing. As to the two titles whose owners have paid out millions in hacking damages to prevent hundreds of other cases going to court: the Mirror managed five paragraphs in a small single on the royals knowing about hacking; the Sun nothing.

And the Mail? Not a word of those key elements from the Harry witness statement. Instead, it led its spread on its own statement, building on the private investigator's recantation, with a panel on the side with his 'point by point' rebuttals of the claims against Associated. It's one thing to get your retaliation in first, but this took one-sided reporting to another level.

Harry vs The Sun

Harry's next action – which he watched by video link – started on 25 April to take on the Sun, which, like the Mail, has always denied phone hacking. This time his central claim was even more sensational: News Group Newspapers owners had paid Prince William 'a very large sum of money' as part of a private settlement to stop him suing for hacking.

This time the story made the splash for the Guardian and the Telegraph, which 'understood' that the figure was about £1m. But its headline wasn't the 'Prince's £1m phone hacking deal' you might have expected, but that the claim had 'left Coronation peace hopes in tatters'. There was, however, a spread inside as well, which was more than anyone else did.

The Times had a page lead and the Express a chunky story on its coronation spread. But the Mail had just a small single-column on page 10 that started 'Prince Harry has dragged William into his war on the British press'. The Sun and the Mirror ran nothing. Royal developments deemed worthy of front page coverage included a chocolate bust of the King and his resistance to having Heathrow's Terminal 5 named after him.

There was more interest the next day, after the judge said he was troubled by 'factual inconsistencies' in Harry's story, with more prominent coverage, including a small story in the Mirror (albeit on a different angle), and an early right-hand page lead in the Mail.

As with the case against the Mail, third day coverage was more limited — the angle this time being Hugh Grant's claim that stars' homes were burgled at the Sun's behest. For the third successive day, the case made the front of the Guardian, a page lead for the Times – and not a single word in the Sun. The Mail may have skewed coverage of its own case for the defence, but at least it was there. The Sun, whose lawyers wanted the case dismissed as out of time, just pretended it wasn't happening and ignored it altogether.

Finally Harry makes it to the coronation — and to the courts

Harry's next homecoming was what the Mail called his 'blink and you've missed it' trip for his father's coronation. He may have gone back to California swiftly after the ceremony, but he hadn't finished with the courts. For just over a week later, on 10 May, a third case started — against Mirror Group Newspapers. And this time it wasn't a preliminary hearing, but a proper trial, expected to last seven weeks. Harry wasn't in court for the opening speeches, but was lined up to give evidence, possibly for as long as three days, in June.

The two key features of the first day was MGN's admission of, and apology for, a single instance of illegal information gathering – by the People – that it said was worthy of compensation, and the assertion by lawyer David Sherborne that it was 'inconceivable' that Piers Morgan was unaware of phone hacking under his editorship. This claim had been made in one of the previous cases and was, indeed, the subject of two identical Guardian front-page headlines.

Morgan, a former editor of the News of the World and the Daily Mirror who now presents a show on Rupert Murdoch's TalkTV and writes a column for the Sun, had (coincidentally?) just recorded an interview with Amol Rajan for the BBC in which he was asked about hacking on his watch. He said he didn't know how to hack a phone (even though he had written about it in his autobiography and is reported to have explained how to do it to a Tony Blair aide), and that he was unaware that hacking had been going on at his papers. He also declared that he wasn't going to take lectures on privacy from Harry and Meghan, who had, he said, constantly invaded the royal family's privacy.

What did our papers make of all that? Apart from the Guardian, only the i and Telegraph had anything on the front, in each case a puff. The i took the 'Morgan knew' line, while the Telegraph went with 'Morgan mocks Duke'. The FT had the earliest inside coverage with a five-column page 2 story headlined 'Mirror accused of industrial scale illegality'. Everyone else pushed the story back as far as they dared. The Sun, Express, Mirror, and Star all went on the apology, while the Times and Mail both majored on the defence line that stories Harry claimed were the result of hacking had in fact been fed to journalists by members of his family and royal courtiers.

As for declarations of interest, the Times mentioned Morgan's current role with TalkTV and listed Harry's other cases against the Press, but did not note that News Group Newspapers shared its ultimate ownership by News Corp. The Mail also mentioned its own case in its coverage. The Sun did not say that it, too, was being sued by Harry. The Express quoted a Mirror spokesman as saying 'MGN is now part of a very different company', but did not add that that company was Reach, owners of the Express (and Star).

Only the Guardian, Times, and Mail bothered to print anything about day two of this trial, when Sherborne told the court that Morgan 'lies at the heart' of the claims. The Times and Mail both led on the Mirror contentions that stories put down to hacking might have been leaked by a Palace aide or the result of an interview with Harry. The Guardian went on Morgan 'approving' the illegal blagging of Prince Michael of Kent's bank details. The reporter allegedly given the assignment was Gary Jones, now editor of the Express. The Times and Mail did not include this in their stories; the Express ran nothing on the case that day.

But nobody reads print newspapers any more. Dead tree news is dead. People get their news online. So what about live coverage on the day the Mirror started? Broadcasters featured it prominently; The Times, FT, Independent, Guardian, and Telegraph all had it among the top four stories on their websites. But scroll as far as you could on the Sun, Mail, and Mirror home pages and you would find not a word. Click on the 'royals' or 'celebrities' tabs and you'd find Kate and George and Charlotte and Sophie, and more Sussex bad-mouthing, but nothing on the trial. Only by searching 'Harry and High Court' did the Mail offer agency reports of the case on a page called 'wires', which has no tab or link from the home page. This is what you call burying bad — or inconvenient — news.

Did any newspaper offer the full story?

By day 44 of this little snapshot, not one single national newspaper had presented to its readers a full and fair account of any of the proceedings in the High Court. The Times and Telegraph came closest, but the rest were either partisan, deliberately blind, or uninterested. The Guardian, which of course uncovered and doggedly pursued the phone hacking saga from 2009 and blew the whole thing open with its Milly Dowler bombshell in 2011, played the cases up – were days two and three of the News UK hearing really worth the front? – while most of the others tried to play them down.

When you have such high-profile litigants taking on the country's biggest news brand — actually accusing its journalists of being criminals — it is worthy of proper attention. When you have a royal prince claiming that the heir to the throne accepted £1m in hush money to stop him taking the second biggest news brand to court, it is worthy of proper attention. When you have the King's son accusing one of the country's most prominent television presenters of overseeing industrial scale law-breaking, it is worthy of proper attention.

If the cases against the Mail and Sun are dismissed at this stage as being without merit, then that tells us something about those people and their characters and motivations and we should have been kept up to speed on exactly what they were alleging, not just given snippets of what the most famous among them said and sniping about their wokeness, hypocrisy, and self-obsession.

If they are rejected on technicalities, then a sense of fair play and justice should allow examination, even without the backing of the law courts, of their complaints. The argument 'It's all navel-gazing, people aren't interested' doesn't wash. Just remember that simple test: what if it had been the BBC in the dock?

There are those who accuse the British press of a culture of omerta, a reluctance to acknowledge, let alone confront malpractice within the 'club', even by rivals. They will be able to cite the Harry coverage in support of that complaint. Regardless of whether they are right, this widespread refusal to face challenges to our industry is troubling. But more so is the fact that it raises the question: if reporting of these cases is so unreliable, what does it say about what we are served on everything else?

Speaking of Harry and Meghan

Meanwhile, the vilification of Harry and his wife continues apace. The day after the coronation, the anti-Brexit author Edwin Hayward tweeted that he had logged more than 100 negative stories about the couple on the Express website in the space of 72 hours. The Sun and Star are withering, the Mail vitriolic, reporting opinion polls that purportedly show the public are sick of them. These papers know full well that the Press has hounded Harry since boyhood and that he blames the tabloids for the death of his mother. But now they brush all that aside as 'other people' and 'all in the past'. It is absolutely in all of their interests to discredit the duke as he stands up to them in court – and they are doing their damnedest to avoid letting their readers know why.

About the contributor

Liz Gerard is a former The Times executive. She monitors the UK daily national press and reports on it acerbically and in depth for InPublishing fortnightly.

Chapter 11

A sick relationship

Professor Julian Petley argues that Prince Harry's legal actions against three newspaper groups represent a very significant departure from the way in which royals have dealt with sections of the press in the past. This is a high-risk strategy on Harry's part. But at the same time the prospect of a member of the royal family who, unlike other phone-hacking victims, appears to be unlikely to accept out-of-court settlements, should these be offered, is one which also carries considerable risks for the papers in question

In May 2023 Prince Harry, Duke of Sussex, was engaged in no fewer than three legal actions against sections of the press: the Daily Mail and Mail on Sunday, published by Associated Newspapers; the Murdoch-owned Sun; and the Daily Mirror, Sunday Mirror, and The People, which are part of the Reach empire. All relate to phone-hacking in the years preceding 2011, when the Guardian's revelations of industrial-scale hacking and private data blagging in sections of Fleet Street supposedly put an end to these illegal practices.

Prince Harry's appearance on 27 March 2023 at the preliminary hearing against the Associated titles inevitably created a press sensation, but it needs to be understood that this is not the first time that a member of the current British royal family has taken legal action against the press. For example, the late Queen Elizabeth sued *The Sun* twice for breach of copyright, firstly in 1988, when the newspaper reached an out-of-court settlement after publishing a stolen private family photo, and secondly in 1993, when the paper published the contents of her Christmas broadcast two days before its transmission. The newspaper paid £200,000 to charity in an out-of-court settlement. And in the same year Princess Diana successfully sued the Sunday Mirror and Daily Mirror for publishing pictures that were secretly taken of her exercising in a gym. Mirror Group Newspapers apologised, settled out-of-court, and are believed to have paid Princess Diana £1m in legal costs and donated about £200,000 to charities of her choice.

What is unique about Harry's series of actions, however, is the prince's willingness, indeed desire, to fight the papers concerned in open court, something which no member of the royal family has ever done before. And the reasons for this reticence throw a great deal of light on the highly complex relations between the press and the royals, and the considerable power that the former wields over the latter.

'Not the done thing'

In Spare (2023), Harry devotes a good deal of space to this relationship, in which the royals and their courtiers regard silence as the best option when the press pack is in attack mode: simply not advisable, just not the done thing, makes our relationship with the press complicated, and so on and so forth. But what also becomes very clear from his book is the extent to which members of 'the Institution', as Harry calls it, are prepared to suffer the worst that the press can throw at them, partly to avoid feeding the beast but also to not jeopardise the more positive coverage that they can engineer. And the famed factionalism within the Institution also performs a key role here, with courtiers peddling positive stories on behalf of their particular faction and negative stories against other factions. Of course, it can be, and indeed has been, argued that Spare is one-sided and partisan (so very unlike the papers which feature in it!), but the picture of Palace-press relations which emerges from it finds a very distinct echo in Tina Brown's more dispassionate The Palace Papers (2023).

The nature of the relationship between the press and the Palace, which Harry describes as 'sick' in Spare, emerged particularly clearly at the end of April 2023. This was in an action involving a claim against News Group Newspapers (NGN), the Sun's holding company, that Harry had initiated in 2019, alleging that the Sun had hacked his voicemails and hired private investigators to blag private information, particularly about his relationships with various girlfriends, during the 2000s. His claim set out over 100 separate alleged payments made by the Sun to private investigators for information on him, as well as examples of stories that he says were the result of his phone being hacked. At the end of 2022, NGN had applied to have the action struck out, on the grounds that his claims were legally out of time, as they should have been made within six years of the alleged offences taking place, and served Harry's lawyers with nearly 1,700 pages of evidence to back up their case.

A secret deal

NGN's case was heard in an action beginning on 25 April. In his 31-page witness statement, Harry claimed that the reason why he had not brought the claim earlier was that, at some point before 2012, the Palace and senior executives at NGN had struck a secret deal whereby the two princes would delay proceedings for hacking in return for an apology and out-of-court settlement when all the other hacking cases against the company had been concluded. As Harry's witness statement puts it:

> There was in place an agreement between the Institution and NGN that we would not engage, or even discuss, the possibility of bringing claims against NGN until the litigation against it relating to phone hacking was over.
> The Institution made it clear that we did not need to know anything about phone hacking and it was made clear to me that the royal family did not sit in the witness box because that could open up a can of worms.
> The Institution was without a doubt withholding information from me for a long time about NGN's phone hacking and that has only become clear in recent years as I have pursued my own claim with different legal advice and representation.

This alleged deal had advantages for both sides. For NGN it meant that details of alleged phone-hacking would not be aired in court, and, most importantly of all, this would enable it to maintain its long-standing claim that phone-hacking took place only at the now defunct News of the World and not at the Sun as well. And for the royals it would, as Harry's witness statement avers:

> [A]void the situation where a member of the royal family would have to sit in the witness box and recount the specific details of the private and highly sensitive voicemails that had been intercepted by [News of the World royal reporter] Clive Goodman. The Institution was incredibly nervous about this and wanted to avoid at all costs the sort of reputational damage that it had suffered in 1993 when the Sun and another tabloid had unlawfully

> obtained and published details of an intimate telephone conversation that took place between my father and stepmother in 1989, while he was still married to my mother.

This was, of course, the infamous 'Tampongate' tape.

Harry alleged that his own family had hidden from him information about press intrusion and that he had been conditioned to accept his family's view that they should not dare to take on the British newspaper industry. He stated, 'The Institution was without a doubt withholding information from me for a long time about NGN's phone hacking and that has only become clear in recent years as I have pursued my own claim with different legal advice and representation.'

Forcing a resolution

In 2017 Harry decided to seek the promised apology from NGN, receiving the backing of both the Queen and his brother William. However, protracted negotiations went nowhere. One of the main participants was Rebekah Brooks, the CEO of the Murdoch's British company News UK, who had been editor of the Sun at the time that the alleged hacking took place. At one point, NGN's intransigence led Harry to consider banning reporters from Murdoch-owned outlets from attending his wedding to Meghan, Duchess of Sussex.

According to Harry's witness statement, by 2018 he felt 'frustrated that nothing had been resolved' and wanted to 'force a resolution' to the phone-hacking business. Sally Osman, the Queen's communications secretary, wrote to him explaining that she was willing to threaten legal action in the name of the monarch. Her email read:

> The queen has given her consent to send a further note, by email, to Robert Thomson, CEO of News Corporation and Rebekah Brooks, CEO of News UK.
>
> Her Majesty has approved the wording, which essentially says there is increasing frustration at their lack of response and engagement and, while we've tried to settle without involving lawyers, we will need to reconsider our stance unless we receive a viable proposal.

But still nothing was forthcoming, all of which inaction Harry traces back to the secret deal above. However, his witness statement also alleges that in 2020 Prince William had secretly been paid a 'huge sum of money' by Murdoch's company to settle a previously undisclosed phone-hacking claim. This has been estimated by the Daily Telegraph at £1m.

Smoothing the way

In 2019 Harry decided finally to launch his own legal actions against NGN, Associated and Mirror Group Newspapers. Significantly he did not use the royals' go-to firm, the venerable Harbottle and Lewis, but Schillings, who have a strong record in representing high-profile complainants against the press. However, he was told by Prince Charles, the Queen's private secretary (Edward Young), and the Prince's private secretary (Clive Alderton) to drop his actions because his father wanted to ensure that the Sun in particular supported his ascension to the throne and, equally importantly, if not more so, Camilla's role as queen consort. In his statement, Harry alleged that:

They had a specific long-term strategy to keep the media (including NGN) onside in order to smooth the way for my stepmother (and father) to be accepted by the British public as queen consort (and king respectively) when the time came [...] Anything that might upset the applecart in this regard (including the suggestion of resolution of our phone-hacking claims) was to be avoided at all costs.

Power without accountability

As a result of Harry's claims, the judge, Mr Justice Fancourt, offered a short additional hearing in the summer. If he upholds NGN's argument that the claim has been brought too late then, subject to any appeal, the case will go no further. If not, again subject to appeal, there will be a full hearing at which Harry would give oral evidence and face cross-examination. As noted earlier, this could prove deeply embarrassing for both sides, and the fact that each is effectively holding a gun to the other's head shows just how serious this situation is. Of course, NGN could offer an out-of-court settlement, but everything that we know about Harry suggests that he would not accept it. Given that he blames the press for what happened to his mother and for making Meghan's life hell, this is obviously a personal battle, but it is also much more than that. As he averred in his witness statement:

This isn't just about phone hacking, this is about accountability of power. Power that informs but is being used to brainwash people. They have created a stalemate society, where they can enrage the public over the most mundane and petty things, to distract from the critical issues for our country and communities.

This is routinely dressed up by the papers in Harry's sights as a spoiled, entitled, and embittered rich kid trying to muzzle the press and suppress stories about him which are allegedly in the 'public interest'. However, as the approach to the press long followed by the rest of his family has succeeded only in entrenching the sense of overweening power and impunity exuded by certain newspapers, Harry and Meghan's decision to tackle them head-on – at considerable financial and emotional cost to themselves – can be regarded as an attempt not only to escape the 'sick' relationship but also to rein in unaccountable press power. Thus the case has ramifications which go far beyond the press-fuelled torments of what Harry calls 'one very large, very ancient, very dysfunctional family (Harry 2023: 399).

References

Tina Brown (2023) The Palace Papers, London: Penguin.
Prince Harry (2023) Spare, London: Bantam.

About the contributor

Julian Petley is honorary and emeritus professor of journalism at Brunel University London. His most recent book is the second edition of Culture Wars: The Media and the British Left (co-authored with James Curran and Ivor Gaber), and he is the co-editor of the forthcoming Routledge Companion to Censorship and Freedom of Expression. He is a member of the editorial boards of the British Journalism Review and Ethical Space.

Chapter 12

Don't mess with John Wayne or the royals: The media, the law, and the royal family

*The relationship between the media and the royal family has always been marred by battles between the right to privacy and the media's efforts to disclose the personal and political details of individual royals. These occasionally culminated in legal action against the media. Here **Steve Foster** chronicles some of the most high-profile cases that have pitted royal privacy against freedom of speech*

The death of Elizabeth II and the start of King Charles III's reign may well herald a new era in the media's relationship with the royal family, with the media benefiting from a more politically charged monarch willing to share political ideas and allowing the media to comment on the political and personal views of the royals. Whether that will materialise, the fact is that when the media have faced legal action from members of the royal family, it has, with rare exceptions, ended up on the losing side, with many decisions safeguarding the privacy and other rights of the royal family also setting wider precedents in this area.

Photographs, privacy, and no public interest

The persistent photographing of and use of the image of the royals has caused a good deal of attrition between the media and the royal family, and no little litigation. The first example comes from the nineteenth century, in a case that did not involve the media, but which illustrated the royal family's desire to protect their private rights. In Prince Albert v Strange, Prince Albert brought a successful action in confidentiality against a former employee who had arranged a public viewing of sketches of members of the royal family, drawn by Queen Victoria and Prince Albert ((1842) 2 De G & Sm 652). The court awarded Prince Albert an injunction to stop the defendant from publishing a catalogue of the sketches, and the case is cited as one of the first successful privacy cases in domestic law (Foster, 2011: 547).

Things escalated with the advent of the paparazzi, with allegations of harassment and systematic intrusions into private life. It could be said that the relationship between the media and the royal family never recovered from the circumstances surrounding Princess Diana's death. Indeed, four years before her death, she brought a successful action against Associated Newspapers, where she was granted an injunction to prevent the Daily Mirror and other newspapers from publishing photographs of her exercising in a gym, which had been taken by the gym owner without her knowledge or consent (HRH Princess of Wales v MGN Ltd and others, unreported, 8 November 1993). This and other cases established liability in confidentiality for the media despite the lack of any relationship between the claimant and the individual taking and selling the photograph — as there was in the Prince Albert case.

This paved the way for general media liability in this area, and with the passing of the Human Rights Act 1998, individuals, including 'public figures' were allowed to use Article 8 of the European Convention on Human Rights to safeguard their right to private and family life. Indeed, members of other royal families have used the Convention to protect their privacy.

Whilst Princess Caroline of Monaco won an action in Strasbourg when persistent photographing of her had gone unpunished in the German courts, no such public interest was found by the French courts when Closer magazine were sued by the Duchess of Cambridge when topless photographs of her on holiday were taken by the paparazzi. The photographs appeared under the headline: 'Oh My God: the photos that will go around the world', and showed the Duchess wearing only the bottom half of her bikini, with more topless photographs on the inside pages. A French court awarded them — a disappointing, according to their lawyers — €100,000 in damages and interest to be paid by the celebrity magazine and two photographers. In addition, the magazine's editor and its publisher's CEO were each fined a further €45,000 – the maximum allowed - in punitive damages (to punish the defendant in addition to compensating the claimant).

Commenting on the awards, the photographers described the judgment as hypocritical, and attacked the 'Anglo-Saxon reasoning' behind the punitive damages. The court also dismissed the claim that there was a public interest in the taking and publication of the photographs, because the public and private lives of the royal couple were so closely linked as to be inseparable, and that it was of public interest to know that future heirs to the throne have a solid relationship and are getting on well. Nice try, but hardly credible given the strength of French laws protecting privacy, and the European Court's clear stance on the taking of intimate photographs, albeit in a public place.

Privacy and royal secrets

In terms of privacy and media freedom, 2021 witnessed the most notorious of the legal battles fought by the royals when the Court of Appeal upheld the High Court's summary judgment against Associated Newspapers brought by the Duchess of Sussex (Duchess of Sussex v Associated Newspapers Ltd [2021] EWCA Civ 1810.) The claims had been brought in misuse of private information and copyright when the newspaper group published articles reproducing extensive extracts from a letter she had written to her estranged father. Dismissing the appeal, and an attempt to adduce new evidence since the first hearing, the Court of Appeal held that the judge was entitled to find that the Duchess had a clear expectation of privacy in that correspondence, and that the contents of the letter were not matters of legitimate public interest. Further, both courts were not impressed by the media's claim that they had reproduced the letters merely to correct inaccuracies in an earlier article published in the United States.

The fact that the case was decided in summary proceedings is strong evidence that members of the royal family have strong claims to privacy despite serving a public role and being in the public eye (and the fact that the Duchess and her husband intended to reap financial gain from future book sales). Furthermore, the fact that the media had broken copyright laws strengthened the claim. This was seen in an earlier action brought by Prince Charles, as he then was, when newspapers decided to publish his private diaries. In, HRH Prince of Wales v Associated Newspapers Ltd, the Prince issued proceedings for breach of confidence and copyright infringement when his handwritten journals to record his impressions and views in the course of overseas tours had been supplied to the newspapers by a former employee of the Prince. The newspaper then published substantial extracts from one of the journals. In this case it was accepted that the Prince had a clear expectation of privacy in the journals, bolstered by a right of confidentiality that had been broken by the former employee. More controversially, there was no public interest in disclosing the content of the diaries, despite them revealing the Prince's views on various countries and governments, such disclosures possibly being in conflict with constitutional convention. In the Court of Appeal's view, there was an important public interest in employees respecting their obligations of confidence, and any public interest in disclosure of the journal's contents did not outweigh the confidential nature of the information and the relationship of confidence under which it had been received.

However, the future King fared less well in 2015, when the Supreme Court ruled that s.53 of the Freedom of information Act 2000 did not entitle Dominic Grieve, the then Attorney-General, to override a judicial decision that information should be disclosed simply because he disagreed with the Upper Tribunal's conclusion (R (Evans) v Attorney General [2015] UKSC 21). In a decision that was more a victory for the rule of law than for the public right to know, the Supreme Court vindicated the Tribunal's ruling, which had overruled the Government's refusal to disclose information sought by a journalist because it reflected the Prince's private thoughts and might well compromise the future King's constitutional neutrality.

Other litigation and conclusions

Despite the victory in the freedom of information case, the general message coming from these cases is: don't mess with John Wayne or the royal family. This is clear from the July 2022 Court of Appeal judgment in Re Will of His late Royal Highness Prince Philip, Duke of Edinburgh , that a judge had been entitled to conclude that an application to have the last will and testament of the Duke of Edinburgh sealed should be heard in private. The judge decided that the entire hearing should take place in private because a series of announcements and a judgment would generate significant publicity and conjecture which would be contrary to the need to preserve the dignity of the sovereign and protect the privacy surrounding genuinely private matters. Putting the press in its place, the Court of Appeal held that it had been wrongly assumed that the media had a legal right to attend and make submissions whenever a party applied for a hearing to be held in private, whereas the media had no such right.

Yet one more victory for the media before we go. In Attorney-General v Times Newspapers, (The Times, 12 February 1983) a court found that a newspaper was in contempt of court when they had written an article asserting that Michael Fagan, who had been arrested for breaking into the Queen's bedroom, had admitted to stealing the royal wine. The press were entitled to rely on the public interest defence, as the revelations formed part of a discussion on the Queen's personal safety, a matter of great public concern. Ah, brings a tear to a glass eye!

References

Rob Evans, Robert Booth, and Rowena Mason (2015) 'Supreme Court clears way for release of secret Prince Charles letters'
The Guardian, 26 May.
Steve Foster (2011) Human Rights and Civil Liberties, 3rd ed., Harlow: Pearson.
Kim Willsher (2017) 'Court awards Duchess of Cambridge damages over topless photos', The Guardian, 5 September.

About the contributor

Dr Steve Foster is Associate Professor in Law at Coventry University, teaching Constitutional Law and Human Rights for over 45 years. He specialises in press freedom and celebrity privacy and the law, and the impact of the Human Rights Act 1998 and the European Convention on the protection of human rights in the UK. He is the author of Human Rights and Civil Liberties (Longman 2011), and has had his work published in several leading law journals.

Chapter 13

Constructing royal soft power: A tabloid tradition

Nathan Ritchie examines the press representation of the first state visit made by King Charles III. Focusing on the tabloid press, he argues that the press relies on an age-old formula to support the monarchy's efforts to exercise soft power

In November 1953, some five months after her coronation, the 27-year-old Queen Elizabeth II travelled to Panama on her first official foreign visit as monarch whilst on a six-month tour of the Commonwealth. This would mark the first time Fleet Street would report on the young Queen's diplomatic efforts as she looked to establish herself on the world stage. The Daily Mail emphasised the overwhelming positive reception she received upon her arrival leading with the headline 'Fifty miles of cheers — THE ROYAL CAR IS MOBBED'. In The Daily Mirror, a picture of the Queen smiling at the crowds as she left Panama with the title 'Sunshine of a welcome!' stressed the feel-good nature of the visit and the crowd's adoration of the British monarch. The impression that the Queen left on Panama was also remarked on years later in 2022 following her death by The Daily Telegraph. This item claimed that the royal visit had left such an impression on the Panamanian people that they were in collective mourning following the death of the Queen.

Find the template and use it, again and again and again

The Queen's trip to Panama marked the first of hundreds of foreign visits the national newspapers would cover over her 70-year reign. Meticulously organised, the events have been an opportunity for Buckingham Palace and national tabloid papers to reinforce the value of the monarch's soft power on the global stage. The organisers of these visits invariably consider the power of the media to frame the occasion as a success and co-ordinate events with this in mind.

These events, which Dayan and Katz (1992) called 'media events', aim to persuade and enlist mass support for the diplomatic aims of the government. Positive media coverage is an essential part of ensuring that the visit seems to develop and progress diplomatic relations, thereby advancing the political aims of the nation. Indeed, the apparently unique capacity that the monarch has to exercise this soft power is one of very few dwindling justifications for upholding the constitutional monarchy in Great Britain and Northern Ireland (Hunt, 2011).

Through emphasising the success of a royal visit and the capacity of the monarch to further the diplomatic aims of the country, the press, in turn, legitimises the existence of the royal family. They validate the monarchy in various other ways including dedicating a disproportionate amount of news copy to even the most trivial of royal activities and acting as if 'the public has an insatiable hunger for royal information' (Billig, 2002).

Yet not all coverage of the royal family is positive, and the British press has a long history of poking fun and exposing information aimed at embarrassing the monarchy. However, in their coverage of royal visits, in particular those made by the head of state, the press rely on an age-old formula which stresses four key points: (1) the monarchy has been welcomed into the country they have visited, evidenced by the presence of statesmen and cheering crowds; (2) they have charmed elite figures and 'everyday people' through unique displays of diplomatic skill and appearance; (3) mutual enjoyment has characterised the visit with a feeling of goodwill upon the monarch's departure; and (4) the purpose of the trip has been achieved with a sense of lasting national unity between the two countries as a result of the monarch's efforts.

Zusammenwirken

Following the cancellation of his planned trip to France due to popular unrest there, Charles's first state visit took place in March 2023 to Germany, the same country as the last official visit of his late mother. The media narrative surrounding the trip was that Charles' visit to Germany would strengthen ties between the two nations after years of diplomatic calamities. Details on the Buckingham Palace website also claimed a purpose for the visit was to highlight sustainability and community. Charles's tasks were to fulfil expectations as the monarch, avoid mishaps, and cooperate with Germany to carry out a predictable and orchestrated event. The tabloids would then do their bit to claim the aims of the trip had been achieved. This demonstrates how the media and the monarchy work together to achieve a kind of synergy (zusammenwirken).

'Charlesmania!'

The Daily Express, which has long been the most jingoistic of the British tabloids, was the only paper to include news of the trip on their front page. It contained an image of Charles receiving a gift from a member of the crowd in the shape of a love heart, whilst grasping a bouquet of flowers in the other hand, presumably also given by another admirer.

The caption read 'Charlesmania! Crowds go wild for 'Climate King's winning performance', referring to his championing of various ecological issues and the supposed popularity this has garnered him among German journalists and the public. Another item in the online version of the paper selected these words from a citizen from Hamburg: "It is a difficult thing for him to do but it's really nice for him to address it. People here feel positively about him, especially his ecological views."

This framing aligned with one of the key purposes of the trip which was to promote sustainability. Furthermore, by employing public commentary, the news story provides the impression that this view is more broadly held by the crowds. It also conveniently defends against accusations that the King's supposed apolitical diplomatic value is tarnished by the various political views he has espoused in the past.

The Daily Mirror also followed the traditional formula of portraying a foreign visit by the royals as successful. Charles is presented as enjoying his time in Germany and at ease with the people. Meanwhile, Camilla is said to have 'bedazzled' diplomats with her 1898 Boucheron diamond tiara. In this, the story evokes similarities between Camilla and Queen Elizabeth II, whose fashion sense and aesthetic splendour was a staple of tabloid commentary. The welcoming of crowds is emphasised, albeit with a more sober report of 1500 schoolchildren and Royal British Legion members, with 'some' holding banners and flowers. The public are described as 'well-wishers' providing the impression that the crowd had come out as an act of compulsion to demonstrate their affection or endorsement for the occasion, rather than simply invitees or people attending out of curiosity or obligation.

Do they mean us/him?

Positive reportage of royal visits often relays positive messages from foreign journalists. The King's speech received praise from The Daily Mirror with one unnamed German journalist quoted remarking that the King 'spoke with great honour'. The story also highlighted the King mentioning quintessentially British cultural products from The Beatles to Monty Python which it is said 'had politicians and dignitaries laughing'. The bilingual turn during the speech to German, which was perhaps its most noteworthy moment, was mentioned in some dailies as an example of impressive diplomatic skill, but the tabloids largely chose to foreground the Britishness of the King and the standing ovation at its conclusion, rather than dwell on his historical family ties with Germany.

The above reporting reveals that the typical criteria used by tabloid journalists to portray the event as a diplomatic success was followed. Charles's unique diplomatic skills, Camilla's appearance, and their welcome by crowds and dignitaries all signalled that the King had done his job well and had been accepted graciously and optimistically by the nation he was visiting.

Other reports explicitly reinforced that the King had proven the worth of the monarchy in terms of its ability to promote the nation on the world stage. An item in The Sunday Express claimed that the visit was a veritable success from a UK diplomatic perspective; according to the item, the King 'crowned an extraordinary month for UK soft power'. Similarly, The Sun described the trip as 'triumphant' and a reflection on 'how much influence he wields on behalf of Britain'.

1953/2023: New monarch, same template?

This has been a brief look at the tabloid reporting of the King's first foreign visit. If one of the primary functions of the monarchy is to exercise soft power and influence diplomatic relations, the press seemed eager to ensure that this perception is continued both home and abroad. They appear willing to play their important role in framing the event as a victory of British soft power by relying on the familiar formula which accompanied so many of the Queen's official travels.

Over time, the British media played a large part in constructing a mythology around the Queen and, at the time of her death, she was seen by many as a diplomat par excellence (Farr, 2023). Early signs seem to indicate that the newly crowned King can expect the same support from the tabloid papers. The actual capacity, of course, for the royal family to change the course of diplomatic relationships is difficult to measure or verify. But this perceived imperative function of the monarch will continue to be taken for granted, supported, and promulgated in British national newspapers.

References

Michael Billig (2002) Talking of the Royal Family, Oxford: Routledge.
Daniel Dayan and Elihu Katz (1992) Media Events: The Live Broadcasting of History, Cambridge, MA: Harvard University Press.
Martin Farr (2023) 'Soft Power and Hard Choices: Royal Diplomacy in the Carolean Age', Britain and the World, Vol.16, Issue 1, pp 1-10
Tristram Hunt (2011) 'Monarchy in the UK', Public Policy Research, Vol. 17, Issue 4, pp 167-174

About the contributor

Dr Nathan Ritchie works as University Teacher in Research Methods in the Criminology, Sociology, and Social Policy division of the School of Social Sciences and Humanities at Loughborough University. He holds a doctorate in British media representations of the Partition of India. His interests cover the intersection of politics, history, and the media, and he has published in the field of political communications focusing on UK and European election campaign advertising.

Chapter 14

Charles III's coronation on TV

Huge national occasions like King Charles III's coronation are, in essence, television events, made for and by the medium. They are the Champions Cup Final for broadcasters. On Saturday 6 May 2023 **John Mair** *installed himself on his sofa and spent the entire day there watching the event on television*

First, just marvel at the sheer size of the UK broadcasting operations for the event. It is mind boggling. Let's start with a few facts. The BBC deployed 150 cameras along the route, in the Abbey, and the day after at the coronation concert in Windsor. Close to 30 Outside Broadcast trucks were used. ITV deployed 70 plus cameras over five productions sites including an RAF base in East Anglia. Sky News used 25 cameras and laid 7000 metres of cable. Some of the cameras, in Westminster Abbey for instance, were pooled, or shared by broadcasters. In essence then the output of the day was the equivalent of 500 cameras. Thousands of UK-based technical staff were deployed, to say nothing of the many international broadcasters and their equipment also covering the event. It attracted an UK audience of 19 million but, worldwide, closer to 100 million plus.

The product

What of the output on my and millions of other screens? Surprisingly similar, though quality varied. If this was a Cup Final then the BBC won but only in extra time. And only just. Their pictures and sound were not as good as ITV's but their stars outshone the opposition.

Canada Gate journalism has become the hard template of royal event reporting: a star presenter in a box with a Buckingham Palace background plus a rotating cast of guests. Kirsty Young, fresh out of semi-retirement, superbly held together the BBC's coverage, her gentle

Scottish voice able to probe deep without the interviewee realising. Tom Bradby on ITV, not so fresh out of his insomnia leave, ran her a close second. He is solid with a smile. Kay Burley on Sky News is not my cup of tea. (To declare an interest, I have directed her in a past life.)

The expert panels

If Kirsty and Tom are the Gary Linekers of this Match of the Royal Day, what of their discussion panels? The crucial difference is that unlike Alan Shearer or Micah Richards none of them have ever played the royal game. Some may feel and act as ersatz royals (no names, no packs drills but Bond and Arbiter come to mind) but does that really qualify them to be experts or insiders? Like most other royal commentators they work on gossip, supposition, and the words of backstairs Billies. They are firmly observers and not former players.

The cast sofa mix can be amusing. David Olusoga, the mixed-race champion of all things Black, shared studio space with Robert Hardman (the surname says it all) of the Daily Mail: no meeting of the minds or the eyes there. Kirsty had a diplomatic job on her hands getting them to connect.

Too many of the younger experts took advantage of the Canada Gate platform to air their views/prejudices (you decide) on slavery, diversity, or any other favourite cause célèbre. At least they look less tired than some of the old ancien regime royal correspondents wheeled out for these events. They normally reside comfortably in the Channel Five or ITN archive Saturday night ghettoes.

Sadly, on days like these, the media likes nothing better than to eat itself. Later in the day, Tom Bradby, current ITV News At Ten host, interviewing Trevor McDonald, the first Black presenter of the programme, represented the nadir of that genre.

Canada Gate journalism seems here to stay. But please can we have better and more imaginative casting. Use those producers in news and current affairs accustomed to delivering guests to sofas and screens with something meaningful to say not ersatz royal family members.

The outside broadcasts

The clue is in the name. Those many cameras are like sub-streams going into bigger streams and eventually into a river of selected pictures for the multi-camera director to select to put to air. I know; I worked on five BBC General Election Night programmes using this hub and spoke system. It is like television Darwinism: the best incidents, pictures, and sound make it through to the viewer, or they should do.

In Westminster Abbey itself the constraints are both ethical and ecclesiastical. The cameras have to be out of sight and out of sightlines and not in a position where they impede the religious element. I imagine the negotiations over positioning of those are tense but precedents exist, some 70 years worth of them.

By far the biggest money shot of the day is that of the camera right at the top of the nave which shows the whole Abbey interior as a cross. It is superb and it was only a pity that the BBC pool director used it just once at the end of the service.

The rest of the Abbey TV programme basically followed the order of service and made sure that cameras and shots were in the right place at the right time.

Music at the coronation is a director's dream and they rose to the challenge. The songs and music were beautifully directed with the right feel and the right mood. Kudos to them.

Since the 1953 coronation the commentator has been the distinguishing factor in coverage. The BBC's Huw Edwards did not disappoint. He had done his homework on the little details that make that interesting but, unlike too many football commentators, was not insistent on spewing out all his research to the microphone. For ITV, James Mates did a competent job.

A coronation without a Dimbleby!

This coronation was the first to be broadcast without any of the TV royal family, the Dimblebys, on royal occasion commentary duty. There was no David in the Abbey but his brother Jonathan was fielded by ITV as a royal expert and friend of the new King. He made a seminal TV programme about Prince Charles in 1994. The 84-year-old David Dimbleby had recused himself, or had been recused by the Corporation. Old age and a tad of criticism of BBC-royal relations may not have helped. In October 2022, Dimbleby stated that the BBC does not appropriately question the power of the royal family. He said that the BBC would not address controversial topics to do with the monarchy, such as its ability to change tax legislation or the fact that the Duchy of Cornwall doesn't pay capital gains tax, and stated his disagreement that such matters were not examined. He also expressed his shock at the amount of control the monarchy have over broadcasting covering the royal family.

Dimbleby is right. For many years the BBC has had a royal liaison officer, a gatekeeper through which goes all communication with royal family. The Palace makes its views known. After the rare success of 1969's Mirzoeff Royal Family programme, the family essentially clammed up, that film lodged in the vaults and future co-operation done only on royal family terms. That oyster stance increased with the War of the Wales and their subsequent divorce, 2019's disastrous Prince Andrew Newsnight interview, and the 2020 estrangement from the royal family of Prince Harry and his wife Megan, and their eventual US exile. In May 2023 The Guardian reported that the Palace had a right of veto over the inserts used on coronation day by broadcasters. In light of this, should the BBC and other broadcasters have agreed to protect the King's modesty as he was anointed, and was the lack of cutaways of Princes Andrew and Harry during the Westminster Abbey service entirely co-incidental? Is the relationship between the BBC and Buckingham Palace too close for comfort?

Social media

This was the first coronation in the age of social media, the forum or gutter of popular opinion or at least those people with a Twitter account. Memes started early with the royalist v republican debate to the fore. One special trope of the day was Penny Mourdant/swords/Game of Thrones. The leader of the House of Commons became an overnight and unexpected Twitter star by her resoluteness and strength in holding two swords of state straight for close to two hours.

Louis, the third child of the Prince of Wales with his impishness, also developed his own twitter meme. Later in the day the Metropolitan Police's crass behaviour towards Republic supporters took pole position.

'The biggest military parade for many years'

On huge state occasions like this the British military come into their own. Indeed they were made for this and for the odd battle. Thousands of them came through Waterloo station - a manna for TV producers filling time before the real parade - to join the royal procession, mainly on the way back from the Abbey to Buckingham Palace. The serried ranks of soldiers, sailors, and airmen (and their horses) from the UK and far flung Commonwealth territories all marching in lockstep down straight avenues made for superb television images, pictures that needed few words. My takeaway image of the coronation military day was hundreds of Guards' bearskins and other hats taken off and lifted in three cheers to the new King on the lawns of Buckingham Palace, all in perfect unison in the rain. The military show-off made the television day.

In other parts of the broadcast wood

My sofa electronic programme guide surfing was by and large confined to British terrestrial channels. Later my fingers wandered across to the new kid on the block or the runt of the pack (take your pick) GB News. Ten minutes with Nigel Farage and his opinions were enough to send me back up the remote control to broadcast sanity. I made my excuses and left.

The after-party at Windsor Castle

Worthy of review too was the event's after-party, the Coronation Concert at Windsor Castle the night after. It was a made for and made by television event. Set up by the BBC, it was a royal Glastonbury with the setting of the Castle to kill for. The Firm turned out in force, seat bopping away. BBC Events pulled out all the technical stops: the event featured a huge round stage which gave information and entertained, links to the nations and regions for the big lighting up the nation, and some simply astonishing drone balletic performances over this and the other UK stages. It was a true television spectacular. The only pity was that the Premier League technology and special effects were let down by a first division performance cast in this strange hybrid of military and pop: Take That with military drummers on stage! A night to remember but for the wrong reasons.

A royal red letter day but also one for broadcasters

There have only been two coronations in the last 70 years. The broadcasters were at both, in 1953 after a struggle the BBC had it to itself, and in 2023 a thousand TV flowers bloomed all over the world. Without the medium there would have been no message from the King to the people.

About the contributor

John Mair is a former BBC, ITV, and Channel 4 producer and director. He helped (down the food chain) invent BBC's Question Time in 1979, and has directed many big events including parts of BBC General Election programmes and G7/G8 conferences. This is the 54th hackademic book he has edited.

Chapter 15

King Charles III's coronation, a stylist's guide

*What did **Peter York** make of Charles III's coronation from his SW1 sofa vantage point?*

The easy option for me on the morning of Saturday 6 May, coronation morning, was to stay in bed and watch it on TV. So that's what I did. Although I live in walking distance of the Palace and the Mall, I'd have to have been waiting since dawn to see anything (better still starting in a tent on the Mall the day before).

I watched some of it. I really wanted to like it, but the early part of the coverage — old people in panto robes milling around in the Abbey trying to be players — made me completely distractable. I checked my emails and messages. I watched my YouTube favourites. I read the paper.

It took forever to get started. And the much-trailed inclusiveness seemed more like pick and mix celebrity culture. Their hearts weren't in it. Meaning occasionally you saw a famous face, but not a patch on, say, the BAFTAs or one of the marvellous old ITV An Audience with… programmes. Broadcasters treat the monarchy as something between old polite showbiz and modest Good Works. Analysis makes audiences turn off. After a while I decided to get up and go out and leave the watching to recorded highlights that evening. It looked much better after tough editing.

Better in the old days, well 1953

Just watch the BBC 1953 Coronation TV coverage (there was no competition, ITV didn't arrive till 1955) and you can see why everything seemed so all over the place this time. This time High Seriousness and low confusion. For better or worse the '53 version was populated by people who all knew each other – and, above all, knew what to wear. There really was an identifiable Establishment. Almost all of them wore long – and that's only the boys! Lords wore their robes, some of them very old, and peeresses wore tiaras. There wasn't room for much debate, or what old Marxists used to call 'bourgeois individualism'. It was also voiced by the marvellously fruity sounding Richard Dimbleby who said delicious things like 'the peers of the realm ... sitting in their lovely robes ... with their ermine capes' or 'the front ranks of the peeresses, their tiaras a shimmer'. In another set of pews sat the bishops, who also knew exactly what sort of long dresses to wear. And in the endless procession of Ancient Britain proceeding up the aisle there were yet more toffs, or rather super-toffs, like the Duke of Norfolk, who had a definable ceremonial role in the whole affair. Behind were their pages, bringing up their coronets.

The new order

'The Firm', anxious to seem inclusive, absolutely ditched the toffs this year, and the whole ancient notion of Lords spiritual and temporal, in favour of a curious combination of styles and looks – including, of course, lots of close-ups. Close-ups with TV lighting are exactly what Walter Bagehot meant about the monarchy when he said, 'We must not let in daylight upon magic' in 1867. The King — actually quite upbeat when he's enthused — looked old and anxious almost throughout, except when the Prince of Wales kissed him and whispered that everything would be all right. It could've been better if he'd done a grand and distant vibe but I got the impression that on this day, when he was making these sacred vows of service to the nation, he was no more certain than anyone else exactly what the precise tone should be, the mix of the solemn and the demotic, Zadok the Priest and the Ascension Gospel Choir.

Are they 'ist'?

Prince William, chased by reporters on 11 March 2021, following up the Sussexes' famous Oprah interview, asked if the royal family was racist said, "We're very much not a racist family". He meant it. It's central to the royal family's post-war definition of their role and mission, to the Commonwealth, to their relevance. But anti-racists as they are, there are clearly impending defections from the monarchy all over the Commonwealth, delayed until the Queen died.

But what if those reporters had asked an altogether cleverer question 'Is the royal family a classist family?' He wouldn't have known how to deal with that one, because the royal family's relationship with what remains of the aristocracy and the assimilated and aspirant plutocracy is deeply conflicted. Clearly they know they can't be seen at the centre of a cluster of coronets. But where exactly do they come from? As clever Ash Sarkar from the very left YouTube channel Novara Media said on Newsnight on 2 May, 'Whatever way you slice it, the monarchy is neither a fair nor representative institution'. But we'd rather have them than Victor Orbán (Hungary) or Narendra Modi (India). All of this is on the table now and everyone is convinced that 'the young' are the crucial constituency deciding the fate of the monarchy (the real demographics show oldies have the power and money in an ageing Anglosphere).

The 'magic of the monarchy'?

The modern need to show diversity, and the need to answer to aspiration and meritocracy means monarchy has a hard argument to make in a close-up world. The precise combination of good works and magic has to be constantly re-thought, decade by decade, while looking like reassuring continuity. (The Queen died two days after receiving Liz Truss, which may have been something of a shock. But I'm saying nothing.)

Just looking at the last coronation shows just how much it's changed – no sign of Arthur Askey or Terry Thomas in the Abbey in 1953. This year Ant and Dec centre stage. And going back to the 1937 Pathé film of George VI's event shows that the following 16 years didn't change things that much. 1953 came before McMillan's 'Never had it so good' speech in 1957, before the 1960s baby boomer culture, and, obviously, way before the Internet.

The monarchy needs to maintain a certain distance while staying relevant, to be that useful bit boring now and then, but not so boring that anyone under 30 — and me — just wants to switch channels.

About the contributor

Peter York is a 'capitalist tool' by background, as a market researcher and management consultant. In parallel he is a social commentator, journalist, occasional TV presenter, and author of eleven books, ranging from the best-selling Official Sloane Ranger Handbook to Authenticity is a Con, an attack on the cult of authenticity. His latest book, co-written with Professor Patrick Barwise, is The War Against the BBC (Penguin 2020). He is the President of The Media Society.

Chapter 16

All perspectives?

When it launched in June 2021 GB News promised to not 'slavishly follow the existing news agenda'. **Andrew Beck** *examines GB News broadcast output in the weeks leading up to Charles III's coronation as well as the event itself to see whether they did set their own agenda*

Once the UK voted to leave the European Union there was much talk, and even more handwringing, about why the 2016 Brexit vote had been won. One aspect of Brexit that puzzled many metropolitan commentators was why so many deprived parts of the UK had voted in favour of it. Why had so many people living in desperately deprived and unhappy parts of the UK, their local governments starved of funding by central government, seemingly voted for more deprivation and more misery? One simple answer is they had precarious or no employment, felt abandoned by London, were unsure about the vocabulary, dress, and behaviour of city-dwellers, felt underserved by London or southern broadcast media. They had been offered a chance to express their opinion and responded with a loud, anguished howl.

That being the case it was a logical move for broadcasters to try to create a TV news channel which would meet the needs of those abandoned people, 'the left-behinds', as they were characterised by Matthew Goodwin and Oliver Heath. Surely this was of a piece with then Prime Minister Boris Johnson's May 2021 announcement that, later that year, a Levelling Up White Paper would be published. He would level up those left behind communities. Where Boris led the broadcasters would follow.

Before GB News began broadcasting then chairman Andrew Neil proposed that it would meet the broadcast news needs of 'the vast number of British people who feel underserved and unheard by their media'. Furthermore, he said, it would not 'slavishly follow the existing news agenda' but rather would reflect the stories 'that matter to you and those that have been neglected'. In a long and noble British broadcasting tradition it would also 'champion robust, balanced debate and a range of perspectives on the issues that affect everyone in the UK, and not just those living in the London area'. And in that spirit of social inclusiveness the GB News parent company was named All Perspectives Ltd.

'Woke watch'

The trouble was as soon as Neil started talking about the channel its position in the ideological spectrum quickly became apparent. Speaking with the Evening Standard's Susannah Butter days before the channel's launch Neil tried to differentiate GB News from US channels like Fox News: "In terms of format we are like Fox but we won't be like Fox in that they come from a hard right disinformation fake news conspiracy agenda. I have worked too long and hard to build up a journalistic reputation to consider going down that route." Despite being at pains to emphasise, time and again, that GB News was not a UK Fox News, Neil then talked about his own 8pm weekday show which would feature a five-minute 'Woke Watch' segment. Neil left no doubt as to his intentions: "Cancel culture is insidious, it stands against everything we have stood for since the enlightenment onwards and that is why it is serious."

The even bigger trouble was that, after barely two weeks of hosting his nightly show, Neil went on holiday. And never returned.

With Neil no longer at the helm any notion that GB News would 'champion robust, balanced debate and a range of perspectives' disappeared.

A shaky start

Early GB News programmes had low, distinctly shaky production values. The studio was part tired 1950s dentists waiting room, part abandoned aircraft hangar, one boom mic suspended over hosts and guests, a grotesque echoing sound, guests ill-at-ease with themselves and fellow guests. Presenters had an incredibly high attrition rate: Dominic Frisby, Dehenna Davison, Alex Phillips, Kirsty Gallacher, Tonia Buxton, Simon McCoy, Guto Harri, Colin Brazier, Mercy Muroki, and Inaya Folarin Iman, amongst many, came and went. As they signed up for the channel many offered a boilerplate interview: 'I'm leaving the BBC/ITV/Sky to break free from their woke straitjacket and to be free to speak my mind'. Remarkably, they all kept incredibly tight-lipped after their departures, with only Neil hinting that his mental health would have been damaged had he remained there.

Nevertheless the channel gradually settled down. Production values improved — in stark contrast to TalkTV, launched in April 2022 and aimed at very much the same demographic as GB News. TalkTV seemed to have put all its launch capital into its onscreen graphics, idents, and Piers Morgan's salary. Programme formats and personnel did settle down. Again, unlike TalkTV (where most programmes are glorified call-ins with shock jock hosts full of opinions, studio guests who agree with the hosts' opinions, and viewers who phone in) depending on when, what, and who you tune in to on GB News there's actually some news.

Its breakfast show now has a settled format, and a stable set of presenters. Monday through Thursday Eamonn Holmes and Isabel Wester present, two guests review the morning's news and newspapers, and regionally based and roving reporters are used. Studio guests are not always distinguished, and sometimes one struggles to recognise people who have long since slipped from being famous for being famous to being vaguely known for being vaguely known. Thursday through Sunday Stephen Dixon and Anne Diamond present, again with a similar format of studio guests, news and newspaper reviews, and reporters in the field. (Although schedules still bill the weekend breakfast show as 'Breakfast with Stephen and Anne', Anne Diamond hasn't presented in 2023. Her seat is most often filled by Ellie Costello, and in GB News' staff profiles Costello is described as a Weekend Breakfast Presenter.) And while it is tempting to view GB News and TalkTV as simply representing two sides of the same right-wing coin (GB News featuring several former Ukip and Brexit party activists, with TalkTV featuring several current Reform party politicians) GB News programme guests are not drawn from one small ideological ghetto. Norman Baker, Paul Embery, Sean McDonald, Jo Phillips, Ella Whelan, and Paul Connew, for example, most certainly do not share the views and beliefs promoted by many GB News evening presenters. (Laurence Fox is in an ideological – and broadcasting – field of his own.)

Putting the GB in GB News

In January 2022, lest anyone should miss the GB in GB News, or think them at all unpatriotic, GB News started playing 'God Save The Queen' at the start of live broadcasting (05:59). After 8 September 2022 that became 'God Save The King'.

Whilst there can be no doubting the political positions of many GB News presenters, Nigel Farage and Jacob Rees-Mogg do have a sound to-camera presence. As the i's Paul Waugh remarked of Farage, he 'remains a formidable communicator with a personal following. His GB News TV show regularly beats Piers Morgan's TalkTV show for nightly ratings'. In December 2022 GB News beat Sky News for prime-time ratings, although not for all-day viewership. The Broadcasters' Audience Research Board (BARB) employs uses a sample of 12,000 people watching TV in 51,000 homes. Their April 2023 viewing figures recorded BBC News at 9,714, Sky News at 7,727, and GB News at 2,811.

So, after a somewhat shaky start, how did GB News report Charles III's coronation?

Other UK broadcasters had screened some royal-themed programmes in the two weeks before the coronation but many of these (The Windsor Castle Fire: The Untold Story (Channel 4); William & Harry: An Uneasy Truce; Charles & Camilla: Against All Odds (Channel 5)) could have been broadcast any time in recent years. Only BBC1's Panorama: Will King Charles Change the Monarchy? (Monday 24 April) or Thursday 4 May's Eastenders ('Coronation fever sweeps across the square, and Billy tries to convince Linda to host a party at The Vic') could have been made in 2023.

Live from Buckingham Palace

GB News stole a march on other news broadcasters by starting their royal coverage on Monday 1 May. That morning anyone tuning in to GB News saw Eamonn Holmes and Isabel Webster on the Victoria Memorial roundabout in front of Buckingham Palace. Granted they did have to keep cutting back to guests in the studio, and yes it was unnecessarily clunky, but Buckingham Palace was there in the background. GB News coronation-related programmes were not restricted to breakfast time either. On Monday 1 May and Tuesday 2 May Nigel Farage's usual 7 to 8pm slot was given over to The Crown — A Thousand Year Story, with David Starkey. Those viewers experiencing Farage withdrawal were relieved to see him back on Wednesday 3 May — for a one-hour special interview with Donald Trump, over in the UK to open his new golf course near Aberdeen. Well, according to Trump, Queen Elizabeth II loved Scotland as much as he did, and on the day she died Newsmax's Greg Kelly claimed that Trump was her favourite US President.

In coronation week GB News certainly got their money's worth out of David Starkey. Not only did he present his two-part documentary but he was also confirmed as one of their three presenters offering live commentary on the coronation, and he turned up as a guest on the Thursday 4 May edition of Andrew Pierce and Bev Turner's mid-morning To The Point show, now also relocated to the roundabout in front of Buckingham Palace. Starkey, back in the studio, was asked by Pierce about UK Prime Minister Rishi Sunak's involvement in preparations for the coronation. Starkey replied that he had been 'invisible', that he was 'not fully grounded in our culture'. Not content with that, he elaborated, "Now I know that's a difficult and controversial thing to say but I think it's true. And again, this coronation is going to highlight far too much I think our differences rather than what unites us."

Not content with fielding guests who did their best to stir up ethnic and religious intolerance GB News also did its best to generate media world controversy. On Friday 5 May 2023, on the eve of the coronation, claimed the BBC had threatened to withhold pool footage of the coronation from GB News, but that, at the last minute (8pm), the BBC 'had backed down', meaning 'viewers across the country can now watch the historic ceremony on their favourite channel'. Never let an opportunity to bash the BBC wokeness, or to bemoan the unfairness, the sheer unaffordability of the licence fee. Even later that night on GB News guests did their level best to stir up more controversy, claiming that all was not well with Charles and Camilla's marriage, and that, once the coronation was over and Buckingham Palace's refurbishment complete, he would live there while she would stay at Clarence House. All good patriotic stuff.

On coronation day GB News' live commentators were Nigel Farage, David Starkey, and Alastair Stewart. Farage and Starkey have no experience of live commentary for this kind of event, but Stewart does, having commentated on the space shuttle Challenger disaster, the Pan Am Lockerbie disaster, the fall of the Berlin Wall, and various UK Budget days.

'Sheer self-regarding arrogance'

The point about TV commentary on royal occasions, just like football commentary, is that it's not meant to illuminate or to shock. Its purpose is to state the obvious: identifying minor royals or international dignitaries viewers might vaguely recognise but couldn't name. Commentators' function is to tell viewers what they're seeing, and what they should be feeling. Even if something out of the ordinary happens their job is to gloss over it and to move swiftly on: nothing must get in the way of the spectacular pageant. As a seasoned broadcaster Stewart knew that, and got on with boilerplate pomposity. Starkey wanted to luxuriate in arcane detail, and Farage wanted outrage. At one point both Farage and Starkey got outrage: Farage boldly announced that he had confirmation of missiles being thrown at horses in the coronation procession. Starkey immediately denounced the protesters' 'sheer self-regarding arrogance'. Clearly Farage and Starkey were as well-informed about what was going on that day as were the Met, who used their barely one-week additional powers to arrest and detain people despite their not having committed any crime. Farage and Starkey's outbursts were then followed by silence, interrupted only by the despairing sounds of their technical crew.

Later that day on his GB News programme Calvin Philips tried to work up a row about whether or not the coronation ceremony was one of faith or of all faiths. The day after Starkey appeared on the roundabout on Coronation Breakfast with Stephen and Ellie saying how much he'd enjoyed the previous day's ceremony: 'I was watching an illuminated manuscript come alive'.

Come Monday 8 May GB News was still on the lookout for signs of outrage. On Dan Wootton Tonight the host succeeded in finding that in other broadcasters' coronation coverage. He began his show lambasting the 'British Bashing Corporation, Woke ITV, and Sly News'. Having berated the metropolitan elite who had been out of touch with the British people's celebratory mood he turned to the topic of racism, and offered a bizarre twist: 'Not one moment was more disappointing than the blatant racism from Bridgerton actress Adjoa Andoh who, for some reason, was invited by ITV to contribute to its coronation day coverage. Probably because she's a well known defender of Harry and Meghan. And, at a moment of history, she decided the biggest takeaway from the balcony appearance was the colour of the participants' skin'. Really getting behind his theme he continued to bemoan the behaviour of Radio 4's Paddy O'Connell and Johnny Dymond, an unnamed Radio 2 DJ, and David Olusoga who 'despises the Commonwealth and Brexit'.

GB News coronation coverage was of a piece with its general output: sometimes chaotic, sometimes professional, invariably patriotic, (selectively) royalist. They couldn't decide on a stance. Attempts were made to perform in a professional, discreet, and respectful fashion (Stewart with all his experience), but the unevenness in the 6 May commentary team soured the presentational style. Farage and Starkey lashed out whenever they found it possible, predominantly at their usual suspects. Ultimately, the early pretence at balance is a far distant memory. Worse still, GB News can't decide whether it wants to be a news channel or whether it simply wants to rage against its own version of a UK Deep State, even as it attempted to celebrate the coronation of a new head of that state.

References

Susannah Butter (2021) 'Andrew Neil: GB News, my war on woke and the problem with Piers Morgan', Evening Standard, 8 June.
Mathew Goodwin and Oliver Heath (2016) 'The 2016 Referendum, Brexit and the Left Behind: An Aggregate-level Analysis of the Result', The Political Quarterly, Vol.87, Issue 3
Paul Waugh (2023) 'A Brexit mea culpa from Farage? More a they-a culpa', i, 17 May.

About the contributor

Andrew Beck is co-editor of this book

Chapter 17

What the coronation papers say

Coverage of the Queen's death and funeral was widely acknowledged as the finest hour for the UK's national press. But how did those same newspapers do on Charles III's coronation weekend? **Alan Geere** takes to the newsagent to find out

Despite the fact that the coronation pageantry was due to be all tied up by mid-afternoon the Saturday papers had no choice to go big and treat readers to the Order of Service: who is going to be where, and details of festivities that may or not go ahead, mostly not in the case of the weather-affected flypast.

The Times fronted up with an ambitious eight-page wrap which opened out into a double-broadsheet spread graphic about the day's events. Newsy 'real' front with THAT picture of Charles grimacing on a walkabout. Intricate flypast graphic across pages 4-5 that sadly ended up being made redundant by the weather.

Page one of the Daily Mirror was given over to a picture of a crown, sorry THE crown. The 'souvenir edition' trundled on to page 19, stopped for a breather, then started again on page 22 with the Order of Service.

A typically incomprehensible Daily Star front page, featuring an Irish wolfhound and sausages, teased to an eight-page souvenir pullout called 'Chas in numbers'.

The Daily Telegraph made full use of the broadsheet format with some huge pictures, plus a monster ad for Boodles across page 2-3 paying the wages. The 84-page magazine 'Charles III, The man and majesty' was a glossy triumph.

The Sun had room on the front for two crowns, a king and queen, and a little picture of Harry (remember him) peering out of the corner. Two pullouts were hidden away behind football and racing inserts.

The promoted '20-page special supplement' in the Guardian was small and thin, rather like the rest of the coverage, which eventually started back on page 16 after old-fashioned news (politics, environment etc). A page of 'What to do if you want to avoid the coronation' includes advice from Alfie of Huddersfield who will be 'knitting in bed'!

Throwback Saturday front page picture in the Daily Mail of Charles at his investiture in 1969 (why? answers to Associated Newspapers, Derry Street, please) touting 'Your definitive guide by Britain's finest royal writers'. Picture-led spreads and neat 'armchair guide' (just like the Grand National) in the centre.

Pretty much the standard front from iWeekend, leading on the results of an 'exclusive survey' which was hiding somewhere inside because there is no crossref. 'Inside: pages 6-17' did promise some goodies, including a think piece by John Sergeant, and 'Best bank holiday wine deals from £6'.

Award for strangest front page went to …The Daily Express with a most bizarre full-page picture of an empty throne, especially odd given the excellent pictorial coverage all the way back to page 19.

I journalism

Forget about those two … it's all about MEEEE!

'I admired the young Charles — and still do' — headline on the Matthew Parris column in Saturday's Times, which also starts 'As I walked to a lecture …'

'I got Charles wrong for years – because I was swayed by Philip…' – piece by 'royal biographer' Gyles Brandreth in Saturday's Mail.

'I shed a tear to watch her crowned queen: the down to earth gal I blew cigarette smoke up a chimney with' — Bel Mooney remembers those party days in the Mail on Sunday.

'I'm so happy for my hero — the king' — Sun royal photographer Arthur Edwards, 82, fulfils a life ambition to photograph the king.

The match itself

In a neat reversal of fortunes with the Saturday papers, that early kick-off at the Abbey gave the Sundays plenty of time to turn around action pictures, commentary, and quotes pieces.

Despite all the real words spoken, recorded, and even captured by lip-reading specialists the Mail on Sunday went for a made-up quote: The look that says: 'Darling, it was a triumph!' Readers were promised 'Breathtaking pictures, the finest writing' in their 'Historic souvenir edition' so a raft of photos took readers up to page 10 and Sarah Vine's overwhelmingly positive verdict.

There was still room for some BBC-bashing, with an underwhelming TV view by Jan Moir of Huw, Kirsty & Co and a news story about unflattering online comments by the BBC royal correspondent.

The Sunday Times neatly tucked away 'all that happened yesterday' in the 12-page 'Dawn of the Carolean Age', only matched by a four-page wraparound that included a full double-truck picture of the flypast. That left the main paper open for a series of think pieces plus 10 pages featuring strips of mugshots of Charles from 1948 onwards. Bravo to the picture researcher and whoever did the picture cropping. Both were brilliant.

In the Sunday Telegraph the 28-page inserted 'Souvenir Edition' is a triumph of photojournalism featuring some of the biggest pictures you ever did see, all printed with precision and that undefinable 'pop' that makes them leap off the page.

Lacklustre choice of page one image in the Sunday Mirror with Charles looking down, either checking his orb is still in place or that Harry hadn't jumped out of his seat. Sixteen-page 'Souvenir special' (yawn) was tucked inside, although don't look for the page numbers because there aren't any.

Serious comment piece from the royal editor as early as pages 6-7 followed immediately by the 'Voice of the Sunday Mirror' greeting a 'new dawn for Britain'.

'Free pullout' in the Daily Star

96 Reporting Royalty

Sunday was eight pages of pictures, including one of the late Queen, not the new one. Good job too, as coronation coverage ends with a dull thud on page seven.

The Sun on Sunday had coverage all the way back to page 33, plus a rainy picture on the centre spread also naming the reporting (17 writers) and picture (14 lensmen. Yes, all men) teams. Sadly no credit for the unsung production team (0).

There was a clunky cut-out of Charles on page one of the Sunday Express (and Sunday People), complete with those podgy fingers, to give a black background which felt more funereal than celebratory. The picture was not even very sharp which gave the whole page a student magazine feel of a Sunday Express pastiche. 'God save the king' was flagged on pages all the way back to page 40.

Their 16-page 'The making of a king' pullout was a triumph of planning with just the cover picture live. It was also a triumph for reporter Mike Parker (last seen in Los Angeles) who wrote every word of the seven stories. Not bad for the scruffy lad who started work with me as a trainee reporter on the Essex Chronicle in the 1970s.

Most opaque headline award to The Observer for: 'It was magnificent, it was ludicrous, and finally this necromancy was irresistible' on page two.

Penny from Star Wars

Penny Mordaunt, the Leader of the House of Commons, became the social and old media heroine.

The old adage of 'if it's a good headline, keep on using it' kept these sharp minds busy: 'The Penny is mightier than the sword' (Sunday Times p10); 'Penny is mightier than the sword' (Sunday Express p16); and 'The Penny is mightier than the sword' (Sunday Telegraph p15).

However, the Daily Star Sunday missed the memo and went with 'Glam Mord is lord of the sword', which some may consider superior.

Prince Harry: here, there, and nowhere

So, the Duke of Sussex duly came and went. Choose your timescale:

'Gone in 35 minutes' was The Sun on Sunday maths on dashing Harry.

'Gone in 60 minutes' was the Daily Star Sunday verdict on 'fleeting visitor' Harry, complete with trademark obscured eyes to protect 'shy guy'.

'Gone in 28 hours and 42 minutes' reported the Mail on Sunday, along with an unflattering picture of him carrying a coat hanger.

A real story amongst the pomp?

A small matter of 62 protesters getting carted away, followed swiftly by a Met Police apology and worldwide civil liberty wailing and gnashing, never looked like threatening to derail the main event.

The Observer was all over it with a page 4-5 spread on the demonstrators with a picture of police wheelbarrowing a purported miscreant away. There was an admirably quick turnaround for a comment piece back on page 47 – 'The police are curbing free speech'.

The protest got a decent show on page six of Daily Star Sunday, complete with picture in the back of a lorry full of confiscated 'Not my king' placards, and a newsy spread in the Sunday Mirror (pages 22-23) with five pictures.

However it was then down to the far reaches of the Sunday Express for 'Early arrests and poor turnout turn protest into damp squib' on page 32, complete with tiny picture featuring 'Not my king' banners. There were six paragraphs of 'Activist arrests' on page 25 of Sun on Sunday and five paragraphs (and two bylines) at the foot of page 11 in the Sunday Times.

In other heckling news, the Mail on Sunday reported on the boo boys at Liverpool FC, complete with a prominent photo of the banner 'You can stick your royal family up your arse'.

Who won the coronation press honours?

Daily Mail Weekend magazine featured a 'majestic cover' created by Andrew Jamieson, the artist who designed the coronation invitation. It was intricate, playful, and an inspired choice by the Mail team.

Production journalists turned around millions of words, trawled through acres of photographs, and delivered memorable keepsakes within hours. Now, where's the food?

The printing was generally superb. Newsprinters, at Broxbourne, who print the Times, Sun, and Telegraph products, reported a combined print run of 3.3 million copies over the weekend, an extra 800,000. Holding the colour on those huge spreads and folding with precision is a skill worth celebrating.

And the winner of the best coronation weekend newspaper was The Sunday Telegraph, which had two sections leading the way with dramatic pictures making imaginative use of every piece of space on the broadsheet spreads and tightly written words conveying the splendour of the day.

My summary judgement

Those of us growing up in newsrooms were used to seeing newspapers — and lots of 'em. Now I'm outside in the free world I don't see as many papers as I did. Yes, I've got the subscriptions and yes, I plunder the 'free' online news but I don't get to see that many 'real' newspapers that often. So this exercise was a delight.

In the rush to digital, online, AI, ChatGPT, and anything else you can think of in the zeitgeist of publishing, the sheer breadth, scope, and let's use the word, majesty of the printed product has become forgotten.

Stand back and enjoy the broadsheet double-page spread pictures which were 40 times bigger than the images I see on my phone (trust my maths, please). Look at the hierarchy of the pages, where bigger headlines guide you around rather than a tip-it-in online template.

Look at how those headlines were crafted to neatly fill the space, ditto the words, not left to drift into online space surrounded by words driven by search engine optimisation. Pictures have energetic shapes and are cropped imaginatively. And remember, this was a one-shot product. There was no luxury of online amendments here.

Lest I get accused of an outbreak of old gittism (gittishness?) the online and some social media coverage was also superb, but these are different mediums – apples and cabbages, if you will.

I am lucky to celebrate 50 years in journalism next year, much of it spent in the engine room of layout, subbing, and editing. There was plenty here to make me want to carry on for another 50 years.

About the contributor

Dr Alan Geere is associate professor of International Journalism at Guangdong University of Foreign Studies in Guangzhou, China. He has been lucky to work in newsrooms large and small around the world – and still does.

Chapter 18

Over there looking at over here (wistfully?)

*Now New York based, **Angela Antetomaso** was a long-time London resident. From her US perch here's how she saw press and television coverage, not only of Charles III's coronation but of his family issues as well*

So, there it was. With a magnificent display of pomp, amid gilded horse-drawn carriages, three majestic crowns, opulent robes and velvet trains adorned with gold and ermine, the coronation of King Charles III, almost 70 years in the making, finally happened. Millions of people cheered around the nation, while thousands of devoted citizens camped under the rain for days, Union Jack flags in hand, hoping to catch a glimpse of the new monarch.

Leaving aside any criticism connected to the astronomical cost of the event at a time of economic hardships for the country (with a reported price tag of £100m), the 1,000-year-old crowning ceremony was a great success. After all, the pageant the British can master when it comes to glitz and elegance is second to none, and that was shown to the world by the global media focusing in unison on the historic day.

The special relationship: so special?

If millions of people were watching in awe around the world, in the United States of America the world didn't stop for the British King. Even the President of the country decided to politely decline to take part in the event, and instead sent his wife to represent the US. I must admit I was a bit disheartened.

Having lived and worked in England for over twenty years, I heard a whole lot about the 'special relationship' between the two countries, and always thought it was a fact. While in Britain, that strong, powerful connection between the UK and the US was sold to me as real, be it by the media, the politicians, or public opinion (i.e. my friends). But now, after four years living and working in New York, where I relocated after the Brexit mess, I realise how little truth there is in that.

With my heart still in London, it pains me to say it, but it might be a mistake for the British to take for granted that all Americans see them as allies or special friends.

When it comes to media, the US press did cover the coronation, but more as a matter-of-fact event than with excitement or passion. There was no closeness or sense of belonging. According to official figures, about 10 million Americans watched the event on TV. That's a huge number, but it's about 3 per cent of the US population. In the UK, over 20 million Britons watched, about 35 per cent of the population. As PBS (the American Public Broadcasting Service) put it, for many nations, 'Charles' coronation is seen with apathy at best'.

God save the Queen/King!

Without delving deeper into the historical reasons for this, and looking back at my years in the UK, I realise now that the lack of excitement might also be due to the fact that, if you have never lived under a monarchy, you don't get it at all. If you never 'had' a Queen (and a well loved and respected one at that) you can't really see the appeal.

As a Londoner I learned to cherish Queen Elizabeth II, her sweet smile and dignified pose, as well as Buckingham Palace, the summer parties, and the Changing of the Guard. I remember the long royal motorcades crossing town carrying the Queen or the Prince Consort, and it was always exciting to be able to get a sight of the royal family.

And then Diana, the 'People's Princess'. How strangely unifying it was in 1997 to mourn her death together with millions of people around the country. A nation in tears. There and then, the monarchy had a meaning. Today? I'm not so sure. And try as she might, I doubt Queen Camilla will ever be loved as much as Diana, the beloved 'Queen of Hearts'.

And finally, Charles. A life in waiting. Whether or not he will be really accepted and respected as a king, remains to be seen. He has got big shoes to fill, and in these ever-changing times it's difficult to envision today's multicultural Britain fully embracing a monarchy that's much in need of modernisation.

Over the years, Charles might have often thought he'd never see the day of his crowning, but when he finally did, he looked quite sombre. It might have been the tension of the special day or the unknown of what it will now be, but this time he couldn't escape the hours-long scrutiny of the world.

This time, all eyes were really on Charles and his newly crowned Queen. At least Camilla, to her merit, graciously smiled throughout the whole event, probably still astounded by becoming the Queen of England, against all odds (also against the will of her late mother-in-law, whose 'sincere wish' was for Camilla's title to be Queen Consort).

And this one time Meghan was not there to steal the show, and possibly endure that dazzling public gaze herself.

Harry on his island and the 'car of shame'

In the end Prince Harry showed up alone, leaving behind his wife and kids. An official statement from Buckingham Palace read, 'The Duchess of Sussex will remain in California with Prince Archie and Princess Lilibet', but many expected Meghan to show up unannounced. Coronation day was also Archie's fourth birthday, and in a way this was a good reason, or excuse, for Harry not to overstay his welcome. He came and went, in a matter of hours — 28, to be precise, as the tabloids pointed out.

This time, Harry flew solo, not only on the British Airways commercial flight that took him home on time to kiss Archie goodnight on his special day, but also at the coronation. Harry walked into Westminster Abbey alone. He didn't don royal attire or a full army uniform despite serving in the Army for a decade. He just showed up in a black Dior morning suit with coattails. An honorary cross around his neck and medals on his chest, Harry sported a light smile on his face, well aware of the intense scrutiny of his every gesture. He sat in the third row, along with his cousins and his uncle Prince Andrew, his face half-concealed by the feathery hat of his aunt Princess Anne, who was placed in the second row just in front of him.

That must have been quite the day for Harry, who had to take it all alone. The usual stares at and speculation about him and his wife were now entirely concentrated on him only, on his every single gesture, word and facial expression, to possibly detect his dismay at not being in the front with his brother, or his scorn at having to arrive in the so-called 'car of shame' (according to The Times) with his disgraced uncle, the Duke of York.

Even professional lip-readers were at work, paid for by the tabloids, trying to decipher every word Harry uttered. But no, he didn't seem to say anything significant, and apparently there was not a word shared with his heir-to-the-throne brother Prince William, nor any evident sign of acknowledgement between the two royal siblings.

To his credit, Harry actually looked more relaxed than the situation allowed. Sitting in the back, quite far from his direct family, Harry might have felt more of a commoner, but after all that's what he chose to be. Those couple of hours in the Abbey might not have been easy, but that was the actual deal he made in 2020, when he chose to leave behind the royal life and its privileges and duties.

Even so, the British media was ready to depict Harry as a 'sad figure', lonely and totally 'out of place'. And not only the tabloids. The Times was ruthless as well, stating in one of its crudest commentaries, 'The King's second son looked alone, tired and miserable. Almost naked in his thin black suit'. The Times also added, after Harry's quick departure, 'And just like that, he vanished: the Royal that never was'.

I appreciate that many people may get so used to this type of language that they become quite numb and don't even notice any more, but is this really OK?

I suppose that moving overseas allowed me to have a more detached perspective that's not necessarily in line with the widespread opinion (and bias) of some of the mainstream British media. I am now struggling to find this type of commentary acceptable, especially coming not only from the tabloids but also from The Times.

Give Harry some respect!

Looking from abroad, I was honestly quite taken aback by the disrespect and the outpouring of hostility toward someone who is still a member of the royal family, and always will be, undoubtedly, the son of the King of England.

Where does this animosity stem from?

Surely Harry and Meghan's way of addressing family issues by opening up to the US media, and washing the family's dirty clothes in an explosive memory book, didn't help. But which came first? The stalking, the phone-tapping, and the venomous attacks, or the Sussexes' reaction?

To my surprise, some of the coverage in the Commonwealth media was also quite harsh.

The Sydney Morning Herald reported that Harry, entering Westminster Abbey solo, 'was his own island'. The Indian Express portrayed

Harry as 'the odd man out' at his father's coronation. The Hindustan Times spoke of him as being now 'relegated to the out-house' by his royal relatives, adding that he 'looked lonely, with a fake smile and ignored by family'.

Now, I have no particular interest in Harry or Meghan but I can't really see how all this could be tolerated, and why it should be considered normal for some press to do this. And I am not alone: not many people in the US really get this vicious behaviour either.

In the rest of the world, the coronation's comments were about King Charles and Queen Camilla, and the cost and pomp of the pageantry. Needless to say, the Waleses and their impeccable kids also attracted great attention, but very little was said about Harry, and Meghan's absence was hardly mentioned.

Only now I realise that that this biased narrative is not widespread all around the globe, but rather confined only to what seems to be the King's own realm. The rest of the world doesn't seem to pick up on that hostility. And in their new home in America, Harry and Meghan are well respected.

Why is Harry in exile?

I don't think many people ever tried to understand the reasons behind Harry's choice in the first place. If a (previously) much-loved member of the royal family felt compelled to leave everything behind — and to give up his title, his riches, and his privileges, and start a new life thousands of miles away across the ocean — there might possibly be a serious reason for it.

And after what I saw on coronation day, I wonder whether there was simply a need to flee from something behind Harry's decision to relinquish his royal title and position, very likely from that intrusive, obsessive treatment that that same press had reserved to his mother, that in a way also led to her death. Love him or loathe him, it takes some courage to walk out of royalty.

On the other hand, unquestionably it could be quite disruptive for the British monarchy to embrace, as full member of the family, a foreign biracial divorcee. That's unconventional, and (partly) unprecedented. But so is Camilla becoming Queen after a dubious start, and Prince Andrew keeping some of his privileges after his many improprieties.

After all, the above is just a sign of the changing times, and embracing it all would be a powerful step towards that modernisation of the monarchy craved by so many, and it would definitely strengthen and benefit the King Charles.

Now more than ever, God save the King. And possibly his broken, divided family.

About the contributor

Angela Antetomaso is a journalist, TV anchor, and host with two decades of live broadcasting experience. She has lived in Rome, London, and New York, working at CNN, Bloomberg TV, CNBC, and Forbes.

Chapter 19

Do they mean us? How the international press reported Charles III's coronation

The world's press says the United Kingdom is good at pomp and ceremony. But was there more to the coronation that just that? **Raymond Snoddy** reads the worldwide runes

After deluging the UK with special, historic, souvenir royal supplements devoted to the Coronation of King Charles III, the British press went on to highlight the anniversary of the great event – the first week anniversary!

On Saturday 13 May, just one week after the event, the coverage continued with yet another official royal portrait of 'three Kings', Charles, his son William, and grandson George, which once again made the front pages.

The Sun managed yet another 24-page souvenir issue while the Daily Mail was offering an exclusive souvenir coronation plate for £12.99 (plus £2.50 postage).

Remarkably the royal coverage staggered on to the Sunday after the week before with almost all the Sunday Times magazine devoted to pictures of the coronation of King Charles III in pictures.

The Eurovision song contest, won by Sweden, turned into another royal media opportunity as the Princess of Wales played the piano with last year's winners Ukraine's Kalush Orchestra in a film that opened the competition.

The coronation was watched by around 20m people on the day, about 7m fewer than the funeral of Queen Elizabeth. Curiously, King Charles attracted the same estimated number as the coronation of the young Queen in 1953 when television – in black and white - was in its infancy with groups watching the 2.5m TV sets out there.

Over there

There was considerable interest in the coronation of King Charles around the world with, for example, all the US networks, including Fox, ditching their schedules to carry the event in London live. The US was also an example of the sometimes ambivalent coverage of the coronation and the current state of the monarchy in the UK.

Many other countries saw what they wanted to see in the spectacular pageantry from Westminster Abbey where British kings and queens have been crowned for close to 1,000 years and viewed the significance of it all through the lens of their own political imperatives.

In the US, the contentious note, mostly missing from the UK coverage, apart from the very special sub-plot of Prince Harry and his lone 24-hour visit, came mainly from the New York Times and the Washington Post. The Post, while acknowledging a back to the future experience, and a 'spectacle of stunning scope even for a nation known for putting on pomp and pageantry at scale', warned however that once the magic moment was over 'such an overtly religious and grand production might ultimately stoke debate about royal wealth and the value of a hereditary monarchy'.

Procession in a golden coach is hard to square with a cost-of-living crisis particularly for a younger generation who appear generally apathetic about the future of a constitutional monarchy. The coronation is estimated to have cost £100m at a time of falling living standards in the UK with new records for the number of food banks being established all the time.

The New York Times, which earlier published an article asking 'why so many nations in the King's realm want to say goodbye', noted on the day that King Charles 'arrived with little fanfare and cringing discomfort'. It went on to contrast the overwhelming regard in which Queen Elizabeth was held with the prospects for her heir who have been waiting in the wings for more than 70 years.

'He doesn't have the long-earned affection or celebrity (as his mother) and he may not have time to build either,' said the Times in a note that was both tart and true.

The Fox News coverage was fronted by Piers Morgan, arch critic of Meghan, Duchess of Sussex, as part of a reported £50m multimedia deal with Rupert Murdoch.

100-million-pound Poms

The controversy over the role of the monarchy came to the fore in

Australia where King Charles III remains head of state, at least for now.

Newspapers such as the Sydney Morning Herald and its sister paper The Age in Melbourne provided extensive coverage but the tensions were all too apparent in the programming of ABC, the Australian national broadcaster. Monarchists accused ABC of 'despicable' coverage that was biased against the monarchy, mainly because of a two-hour special that looked at how relevant the monarchy now was to the lives of Australians.

Only a quarter of the panellists were seen as monarchists, and considerable emphasis was given to the views of the indigenous Aboriginal population and the impact of colonisation on their history and lives.

The Australian Prime Minister Anthony Albanese hoped that King Charles and Prince William would visit the country soon but said he still wanted an Australian to be the country's head of state. This ambivalence was further symbolised by the decision not to light up the sails of the Sydney Opera House, as it did to mark Queen Elizabeth's death, on grounds of cost.

In New Zealand Prime Minister Chris Hipkins, a Republican who was a guest at the coronation, admitted that there was no groundswell of support for constitutional change.

The place we used to call Europe

In Europe there was enormous interest in the coronation, particularly noticeable in countries which have not had monarchies for centuries.

Coronation coverage in French newspapers was very positive including the thought that the monarchy gave a Britain that was more isolated after Brexit the benefit of soft power, which remained a palpable force. As Le Monde put it: 'Even after Brexit British soft power still appears to work perfectly when it comes to attending a royal event.' Le Figaro described the ceremony as a 'coronation to celebrate the unity of the Kingdom' while Le Point suggested the ceremonial 'illustrated the new sovereign's assertive style of bringing together tradition and modernity'.

They still love a good coronation in Italy even though their last King Umberto II, tainted by his association with fascism, went into exile in 1946, and the Savoy line of Italian kings effectively came to an end 20 years ago when Victor Emmanuel renounced his claim to the throne. It appeared extraordinary that the Rome daily Il Messaggero gave up its first five pages to a coronation in another land.

As The Times (London) reported, TVE, monarchist Spain's national broadcaster showed a four-hour special programme, while the El Pais newspaper aptly described the coronation as 'modernity, in moderate doses, mixed with pomp and tradition'.

The conservative newspaper ABC stirred in the UK Government's heavy local election losses in England that came just before the Coronation with the headline: 'Charles III big day eclipses the Tory debacle'.

There was also extensive coronation coverage in the German press with most large media groups also highlighting the arrest of 52 anti-monarchy protesters who did not in the main get to do much protesting, which later led to some Metropolitan Police 'regrets' if not actual apologies. German newspapers also noticed the lady with the sword – Penny Mordaunt, Lord President of the Privy Council who held a 3.8 kg sword up for nearly an hour.

Back in the UK that feat of arms led the Daily Mail and The Daily Telegraph to ponder whether this made Mordaunt once again a contender to lead the Conservative party.

Imperial candour? Old and new

Asia in general appeared to be less excited about the coronation although it was noted in India how many people of Indian origin were in the audience, not least the British Prime Minister Rishi Sunak.

In former British colony Sri Lanka the Colombo Telegraph concluded that if the Monarchy in Britain were to wither away 'it would be more on account of the excessive indulgences of the Royal Family than due to any resentment among or revolt of the British people'.

Across Africa, according to The Guardian, reactions were mixed. There was pleasure that South Africa soprano Pretty Yende had sung at the opening of the ceremony. There were also calls from left-wing groups for the return of the Star of Africa, the world's largest diamond which is set in the royal sceptre held by the King during his coronation.

In other African countries there was considerable emphasis on the colonial past. In Kenya political analyst Herman Manyora said many people had been put off by 'the torture during colonialism, because of the oppression, because of detentions, because of killings, because of the alienation of our land'. In Uganda there was an interesting comment from political commentator Asuman Bisiika who suggested that British culture continued to have a strong influence on young people in Uganda, particularly among those who follow Premier League football. 'It's not about caring for the Monarchy. It's about relating,' Bisiika argued.

The approach of RT — Russia Today — which lost its licence to broadcast in the UK in 2022, was entirely as expected. It concentrated on what it saw as a growing Republicanism in the UK and on the arrests of would-be protesters, a propaganda gift for a state-controlled broadcaster such as RT.

Cargo cults (Prince Phillip version)

In what could not have been a greater contrast the people of Tanna, a volcanic island that is part of Vanuatu, celebrated enthusiastically with a feast, dancing, and drinking shells of kava. They believed that the late Duke of Edinburgh was a deity who they believe came originally from Vanuatu. The villagers have been presented with a portrait of the new king and although they have expressed themselves happy with King Charles III it is so far unclear whether they regard him as a God or not.

Away from myth, the interest from much of the rest of the world for a coronation in the UK is remarkable by any standards. Rarity value contributed something of the allure, given there hasn't been one for 70 years. Mainly it is about the history and continuity and the fact that Britain does pageantry in the Abbey on the march with inch-perfect orchestration. Already there have been suggestions that King William's coronation, when it comes, could be a very different scaled-back affair. If that were to happen it might also be much less attractive as a worldwide media phenomenon.

About the contributor

Raymond Snoddy OBE is the former media editor of The Times and the Financial Times. His publications include: The Good, the Bad and the Unacceptable: the Hard News about the British Press (Faber & Faber 1993), Greenfinger: the rise of Michael Green and Carlton Communications (Faber & Faber 1996), and It Could Be You: the Untold Story of the National Lottery (Faber & Faber 2001). He is now a freelance writer.

SECTION THREE
The end of the line?

Introduction
John Mair

Finally let's look at some of the big problems which the British royal family (and the media) will face after Charles III's coronation.

What is the point of it all? Times columnist Sir Trevor Phillips is a child of the Commonwealth, educated in his parents' land Guyana. A distinguished television journalist, he feels that his fellow scribblers have missed many big questions raised by the coronation. In 'Some basic questions about the media and the monarchy' he ends by saying, 'Perhaps, before asking what the royalty is for, we need to remind ourselves what the media's purpose in a modern state is; if it is to help the citizen understand the role of the monarchy in modern times, we still have much work to do'.

Marcus Ryder, who is of Jamaican heritage, is more radical than Sir Trevor. Marcus is a former senior BBC executive, now leading the Sir Lenny Henry Centre for Media Diversity at Birmingham City University. In 'Royal coverage: Not holding power to account' he argues that the answer lies in newsrooms better representing the Rainbow nation that is the UK today: 'The coverage of the King's coronation cannot be viewed in isolation. Seen in the wider context of the Queen's death, the King's ascension, and coverage of the royal family generally, it offers important lessons as to why diversity and inclusive representation are essential to good journalism'.

Paul Connew is white British. A former senior editor on tabloid papers like the News of the World and the Sunday Mirror, Mirror Group US Bureau Chief, and now a go-to media commentator. In 'Standing at the coronation crossroads' he starts with a confession, how he has moved from 'a lifetime of (lukewarm) monarchist to the brink of (lukewarm) republican'. Closely examining print media coverage of Charles III's coronation, against a background of the current state of the UK, and informed by official public opinion polls as well as his own informal polling of young people, he concludes that 'the media was performing a symphony of sycophancy'. And this spectacle played especially badly if one considers how 'no other surviving European monarchy bothers with such an extravaganza'.

Before some outright dissent it's time for some more history. In 'Irish republicanism and the monarchy' Dr Steve McCabe of Birmingham City University argues that the seeds of hate planted by centuries of British colonialism in the North of Ireland may just not bear fruit thanks to the use of 'soft power' by the British royal family: 'Though Charles III surely recognises that being a monarch who is as universally respected and admired as his mother by all communities in Northern Ireland is no easy matter, he's made a decent start'.

Finally some full blooded republicanism. Originally from Bradford Phil Butland is a member of The Left Berlin, a community of international progressives who run an online journalism project as well as collaborating on campaigns and events. In a coruscating piece prompted by the death of Elizabeth II, he argues strongly against the monarchical role of hereditary plutocrats (of German origin) in contemporary Britain. He looks on in horror at the way in which any number of supposedly left or left-leaning individuals and organisations all appeared to forget their principles when the Queen died. When reading apparently progressive British newspapers he also finds them wanting. In 'The Queen is dead; republic now!' he is not kind to the queen of British liberal journalism: 'Shortly after Elizabeth's death the Blairite journalist Polly Toynbee wrote an egregious piece in The Guardian in which she stated, "Every nation needs a figurehead; and, however perverse the sheer randomness of being born into that role, she did it with remarkable skill and dignity". In other words, know your place, plebs.'

But how do the British public feel about the monarchy? In his Afterword, Sir John Curtice of Strathclyde University, the UK's best known and most trusted psephologist, reads the opinion poll results over many years. In 'From consensus to contention: Changing attitudes towards the monarchy' he traces a history of fluctuating public support for the monarchy, citing March and April 2023 polls that suggest 'a little under three in five now support the monarchy, while one in four would prefer an alternative. While the crown is still popular, its merits and demerits have now become the subject of media commentary and public debate'. But he concludes all is not necessarily lost as far as the British royal family is concerned: 'The public appreciation of the late Queen's visits to Ireland a decade ago suggests the monarchy's future lies in wielding its 'soft power' to bring people together at home and to project Britain's image abroad - including well beyond a Commonwealth whose own ties to the monarchy may soon be few and far between. If the 'mystique' of the monarchy is to be preserved, it will need to be used to good effect.'

So King Charles III's coronation may have been so much pomp and ceremony and 'brought the nation together' according to much of the British media, but it also forced the UK to ask itself some serious questions about the monarch and the media and their at times healthy, at other times unhealthy relationship. Hence this book.

Chapter 20

Some basic questions about the media and the monarchy

The crowning of Charles III was comprehensively reported. That coverage prompted **Sir Trevor Phillips** to ask some fundamental questions about the British monarchy, the British, media and their relationship

Few issues test the craft of journalism more keenly than coverage of the British royal family; the recent coronation provided a lens through which we can assess the health of our trade. Our job is to add to the understanding of the citizen by reporting comprehensively, independently, and dispassionately; and to offer insights that those not paid to opine, and too busy to think deeply about the future OF the monarchy, might appreciate. After the anointment of King Charles III, the best that can be said is that we achieved that outcome patchily. Most of all, we failed to ask the most important question: what is the monarchy for?

On the plus side

There's no doubt that the colour and drama of the event could hardly have been more fully reported. Even media which was self-consciously sceptical about the institution devoted space and time to the preparation, the ritual and the aftermath. Whatever the citizen's taste, there would have been enough pictures, reportage and commentary to satisfy even the most enthusiastic or cynical reader listener or viewer. Undoubtedly, that was driven by the fact that this was such a rare event: it hasn't happened for seven decades and is unlikely to take place for another fifteen or twenty years.

To my own relief, little of the coverage was devoted to the marginal:

speculation about relations between the King's sons and the absence of Meghan, the Duchess of Sussex. It was to the credit of most media that they resisted the noises off from California designed to place the Netflix division of the royal firm in the spotlight. The television reporting was spectacular, and what I saw of the live coverage seemed well-informed. Kudos to my Sky colleague Alistair Bruce (supplemented by the star power of Joanna Lumley) for his thorough immersion in the whys and wherefores of the parade.

On the not so good side

Were we independent and dispassionate? Up to a point, Lord Copper. Most of the noise around the King's supposed unpopularity has died down. No one writes any more about the insane proposition that the Crown might skip a generation – a notion that, however entertaining it might be for daytime talk show hosts, is just nonsensical in the context of an hereditary monarchy, whether one likes it or not. The transformation of Queen Camilla from 'the most hated woman in England' to a book-loving, doughty campaigner for women's rights carries a whiff of media hypocrisy; the woman herself has barely changed, but our fickleness is on full display now that editors know that she'll be there for the long haul and they'll need to get on with her.

The highlighting of the dim-witted police handling of a tiny protest seemed to me to be the media's apology for not being able to find reason to carp at the main event. It is a feature of contemporary journalism that whatever the authorities do, even if they do it well, there must be shortcomings found and focused upon, no matter how disproportionate the degree of attention is relative to the degree of failure.

The republican sabre-rattling of the leaders of two Caribbean ministates with a population of fewer than 150,000 people between them falls into the same category; next time Blackpool or Brighton decides to issue a declaration of independence I expect front page coverage.

The way forward for royalty and the media?

The shame of this is that this should have been an opportunity to get past the personalities and the prospect of republicanism being used as part the negotiation over aid budgets. Little was written or said about the future role of the King. At a time when faith in politics is declining, when the nation is divided in various ways, there is an obvious role for the sovereign, who represents the state rather than the government, to provide a steadying hand and a guarantee of unity. How he does that and whether he has displayed the capacity to meet the task should have been the stuff of serious commentary. Instead, most opinion divided according to whether writers liked the individuals – Charles, Camilla, William, Kate — or not.

Sadly, in the welter of opinion that treated the coronation as a souped-up version of Strictly Come Dancing we saw, heard, and read little about the role of the monarchy in our democracy. Perhaps, before asking what royalty is for, we need to remind ourselves what the media's purpose in a modern state is; if it is to help the citizen understand the role of the monarchy in modern times, we still have much work to do.

About the contributor

Sir Trevor Phillips CBE is a columnist on The Times, presents political programmes for Sky News, and is vice-president of the Royal Television Society. He was head of current affairs at London Weekend Television, and has made programmes for both BBC and Channel 4. He was head of the Commission for Racial Equality (CRE), and its successor organisation, the Equality and Human Rights Commission (EHRC), from 2003 to 2012.

Chapter 21

Royal coverage: Not holding power to account

When it comes to royal reporting **Marcus Ryder** *sees the British media as being too compliant*

Back in 2012 the then Duke and Duchess of Rothesay, better known as Prince Charles and Camilla, visited the BBC Scotland Studios in Glasgow to celebrate 60 years of BBC Scotland television. I was head of BBC Scotland Current Affairs programmes at the time and I was duly lined up with other executives in the newsroom to greet them and say a few words about the work we do. After they met staff in the newsroom they filmed a special edition of the weather report in which Charles and Camilla took turns in presenting the forecast.

What I remember most about the royal visit was not what happened on the day but what happened the day after.

The following day Scotland's then First Minister, Alex Salmond, came to the Glasgow studios and was also given a brief tour. The difference between how the BBC news executives dressed and acted on the two days was marked. On the first day BBC executives greeted the non-elected king-in-waiting dressed in evening suits and ties for the men, and formal dresses for the women. On the second day the same BBC executives meeting the highest elected official in Scotland had reverted to jeans and trainers, and the few who were wearing suit jackets were definitely not wearing ties.

Royalty suits them?

Although my BBC colleagues were fastidious not to discuss their own personal politics at work (the idea of impartiality runs deep in BBC newsrooms) I personally knew that some of the BBC news executives were royalist and others were monarchists. I also knew that there were SNP supporters among them as well as well as supporters of other political parties. But irrespective of people's personal views the overriding culture on display was one in which you showed deference and respect to royalty and relative indifference to elected officials, however high their office.

As one of the few Black people of West Indian heritage working at senior level at the BBC I was more than aware of the ongoing debate that was taking place in the Caribbean about the role of the monarchy. Kenya became a republic in 1964; being married to a Kenyan I understood that Black British people have a very different historical relationship with the royal family. While it's easy to dismiss fashion choices, the different treatments troubled me, to say the least, as to what it said about the prevailing cross-political culture in the newsroom and who shaped it. For the record, for both visits I dressed in the same smart casual way I usually did every day in the office.

I was reminded of these different treatments recently when I found myself in a discussion with senior news executives from both newspapers and television on how different news outlets had covered the Queen's funeral.

I said that I thought the domestic coverage in general, and the BBC's in particular, had been unduly uncritical of the monarchy when one compared it to news coverage elsewhere in the world. The response I received from several executives in the (virtual) room was that the British broadcasters 'couldn't have reported on the Queen's death in any other way' without being disrespectful, and the period directly following the queen's death 'was not the time to be critical'.

Second time round more critical?

There is little doubt that news coverage of the role of the monarchy in Britain has been more critical and questioning in the run up to the Charles III's coronation than during coverage of the Queen's death. For example, three weeks before the coronation, BBC Panorama broadcast a programme titled 'Will King Charles Change the Monarchy?' The programme shared poll findings that only a minority of people under the age of fifty positively preferred a monarchy to an elected head of state, yet overall 58 per cent of people preferred an unelected monarchy to an elected head of state. BBC Radio 4 also broadcast 'The Today Debate: Do We Need a Monarchy?' And other UK broadcasters have had similar programmes critically analysing the role of the monarchy as an institution in UK life and politics.

However, far from making up for a lack of critical coverage during the period of the Queen's death, all this new coverage highlights a serious journalistic failing.

To use a simple analogy; if the position of King was an elected one, the critical debate and polls around the monarchy now, at the time of the King's Coronation, feels like having election coverage after all the votes have been cast, the winner has been announced and we're just deciding where to hold the victory celebrations.

Why? That's because the period covering the Queen's death was also the same period as King Charles III's proclamation and ascension to the throne.

It is that time, not now, that was the critical time in which British journalists should have been asking the difficult questions about the monarchy and fulfilling one of the fundamental principles of journalism, 'holding power to account', however inconvenient or unpopular among certain sections of society that truth might have been. It was that time, that was the decision point for the public.

Instead, far too many news organisations and journalists seemed to be caught up in the narrative that we were a 'nation in mourning', and therefore actively discouraged coverage that was critical of the monarchy.

Groupthink and lack of diversity in the gatekeepers

I believe the reason this was able to happen was because the senior editors, those with decision-making power, are not diverse, and therefore subject to group-think, even if they are critical of the monarchy in theory in practice and culture they are extremely deferential (think of the way my BBC Scotland colleagues dressed for the royal visit).

The fact is, as a person who analyses media diversity, I am always suspicious when the UK is ever portrayed as a nation with a single homogeneous position or view on anything.

The UK is by definition a heterogeneous country (the clue is in the name United Kingdom) made up of four nations: England, Scotland, Wales, and Northern Ireland, and has a multicultural population due to being a former empire. The four nations, those with heritage from the former colonies, and, interestingly, different age groups, have very different relationships with the monarchy. The poll commissioned by Panorama at the time of the coronation only reinforced what previous polls had previously indicated.

What the people think?

A May 2022 poll by the British Future think tank indicated that only 45 per cent of respondents in Scotland positively wanted to retain the monarchy, with 36 per cent saying they thought the end of the Queen's reign should mark the end of the monarchy altogether.

The same British Future poll showed only 40 per cent of 18-to-24-year-olds supported keeping the monarchy, and only 37 per cent of people from an ethnic minority did so. In 2021 a similar poll conducted by Panelbase found that 47 per cent of Scottish adults would vote to keep a royal head of state, compared with 35 per cent who were in favour of an elected head of state.

The story becomes even more complex once age is combined with regionality. According to a YouGov poll, also conducted in May 2022, 80 per cent of 18-30 year olds in Wales want to abolish the monarchy.

What these polls, taken well before the Queen's death, before the King's proclamation, and ahead of the King's coronation, showed is that there is a sizeable section of British society that do not want the monarchy to continue. The further you go from a White English, middle-aged bias, the larger this minority becomes and is even a majority in certain demographics.

Et voila, not coincidentally, it is exactly the demographic that most supports the continuation of the monarchy who are disproportionately in positions of editorial responsibility in our newsrooms.

Did the UK media reflect public opinion?

Irrespective of how well the news media has now been able to cover these opinions at the time of the ceremonial coronation, the failure to cover them impartially at the critical time of the King's proclamation (and the monarchy's continuation) has two serious consequences.

Firstly, it eroded the already limited trust certain demographics have in the mainstream media. At critical national moments it is vital that the whole country is represented in all its diversity. It is not good enough to say the media will only represent the whole country's views when it is more 'convenient' or deferentially 'appropriate' to do so. That erosion in trust can push already marginalised groups, even if they are the majority, to less reputable news sources on social media that might be more prone to misinformation.

One only had to take a cursory look at #BlackTwitter or #IrishTwitter at the time of the King's proclamation and ascension to see a range of British and non-British views on the Queen's death that were not being reflected in mainstream UK news.

Some UK newspapers and other media outlets did, at the time of the King's proclamation, publish opinion pieces by people from Black, Asian, and minority ethnic backgrounds that explained why they were not mourning the death of the Queen in the same way as other people in Britain. However, it is important to realise that this approach was in itself problematic, and further exacerbated the sense of 'us and them'.

This is because it juxtaposed the supposedly 'correct' editorial stance (i.e. that the whole nation was mourning) which had the full weight and authority of so-called 'impartial' journalism with another stance relegated to being just an 'opinion'. Moreover, commissioning these as opinion pieces risked framing any dissent from the dominant editorial stance as a 'problem of the ethnics', i.e. a problem with multicultural Britain, which many parts of the population are proud of.

What at first may seem like a welcome attempt to include more diversity, can instead at best lead directly to sloppy journalism and at worst exacerbate structural imbalances regarding whose opinions are heard and valued in the British national conversation.

The second consequence of the failure of impartially in reporting Charles becoming King was the creation of fundamental misunderstanding about British democracy and rights.

The best example of this was when four people were arrested in Scotland for protesting against the ascension and proclamation of King Charles III. At the time, many newspapers framed it as a 'freedom of speech' issue and about the 'right to protest'. However, the journalism should have presented it as a representational issue. Why?

Assuming the polls taken both before and after the Queen's death were correct, these four protesters were representing the views of over a third of Scottish people.

The four protesters chose precisely the right time to speak 'truth to power' and engage in the democratic process. The newspapers framing it as a 'right to protest' issue essentially disenfranchised large swathes of the population and stifled an important debate. The fact that news outlets are covering dissent regarding the continuation of the monarchy now is literally too little too late for that dissenting voice to have any impact.

Not monarchist, not republican, just impartial

In these emotionally charged times I should emphasise that this is not about being a monarchist or a republican, and as an impartial journalist my own leaning has no consequence. Nor am I ignoring the fact that a large proportion of the British population were grieving at the time of the Queen's death and King's proclamation and ascension. This is about professional and impartial journalism, reflecting an authentic picture of the views and opinions of the entire nation back to itself and fulfilling its critical role in the democratic process of holding power to account at the most important times.

The coverage of the King's coronation cannot be viewed in isolation. Seen in the wider context of the Queen's death, the King's ascension, and coverage of the royal family generally, it offers important lessons as to why diversity and inclusive representation are essential to good journalism.

Thinking back to Prince Charles' visit to Glasgow I hope we can create newsrooms which value our highest elected officials as much as our highest unelected ones. Or at least treat each as critically as each other. More diverse newsrooms would be an important step to achieving this.

About the contributor

Marcus Ryder MBE is Head of External Consultancies at the Sir Lenny Henry Centre, and visiting professor of Media Diversity, at Birmingham City University. A former senior BBC executive with over twenty-five years journalistic experience, including ten at senior management level, he has led diverse teams delivering daily financial and general news and award-winning investigative programmes.

Chapter 22

Standing at the coronation crossroads

*Queen Elizabeth II's Coronation on 2 June 1953 was only the second time schoolboy **Paul Connew** had watched television. The first, a month earlier, was the famous Stanley Matthews Cup Final. The football left the more vivid impression. Both were on his aunt's TV set, the only one in the family. Looking at royal media coverage at the time of King Charles III's coronation and reflecting on what this tells us about the state of the nation, he begins with a confession that would dismay his staunchly royalist parents if they were still alive*

A funny thing happened to me on the day of the King Charles III's coronation. I found myself at a crossroads, taking me from a lifetime of (lukewarm) monarchist to the brink of (lukewarm) republican. Not for me taking to the streets with a placard declaring 'Not my King' but a strong feeling that if this wasn't the last coronation in the UK's history then it really ought to be.

The deeply disturbing evidence that the Met added to its misogyny and racism charge sheet with an excessive, legally questionable, democracy stress-testing crackdown on peaceful Republican protesters warrants comprehensive investigation by the media, civil rights lawyers, the courts, and the independent police watchdog. Sections of the media were slow to focus on this on the day of the coronation, seemingly for fear of raining on the euphoria parade.

Arguably the government's draconian powers move on Public Order and Home Secretary Suella Braverman's rabid rhetoric have created a politically toxic climate that ought to ring alarm bells for King Charles himself.

In the coronation build-up Gaby Hinsliff rather neatly put in her 2 May Guardian column: 'It was the call to swear an oath of allegiance to the king that did it. […] But the idea of encouraging viewers watching the ceremony at home to let out a cry of loyal devotion to the king, in unison with the abbey crowd, something audibly cracked. A public act of homage? How positively feudal'.

The Archbishop's bish

I know exactly what she meant. Polls suggest around two-thirds of the population agree. The oath was the idea of the Archbishop of Canterbury, but was more a 'bishop's bish' despite efforts to repackage an exhortation as a polite invitation. While, in an increasingly secular nation, the coronation's high point, the Anointing (hidden from the congregation and global TV audience at Charles' insistence), with its presumption of God intervening to countenance an hereditary monarch who should 'live forever', strikes many as an arcane excursion into The Theatre of The Absurd. Or, as one young family member put it 'More Game of Thrones than Game of Thrones but minus the dragons'. The nearest things to dragons? The furore in the kingdom of cyberspace about Prince Harry and Prince Andrew. The former's attendance sparked mixed support and opposition, while the latter got an overwhelming thumbs down.

Millions did heed the 'homage' cry, while millions didn't. But feedback suggests that across the nation's hostelries, with drinkers watching the coronation on TV screens, much irreverent merriment was to be had by shouting the oath in the manner of a football chant rather than sober solemnity. Vox pops among the crowds lining the route suggested a cocktail of genuine fidelity mixed with simple big event curiosity.

But what should really be taxing King Charles III, his courtiers and heirs, is those recurring poll statistics. While they show a significantly reduced majority still favouring the monarchy, around 64 per cent of Brits either cared not at all or not very much about the coronation, according to YouGov.

Most worrying of all for Prince William as much as his father, are the polls consistently showing that a hefty majority of 18-24-year-olds no longer support the monarchy at all.

Another poll that will doubtless warrant King Charles' attention is one showing that in six of the 15 Commonwealth states that still recognise him as head of state, clear majorities now favour becoming republics.

Despite the King's ambition to make his crowning glory day a more modern, more inclusive event than his mother's, the pomp and circumstance, pageantry, and expense played badly with millions of young people for whom it was more a celebration of the chance to party with the pubs staying open longer than usual and an extra Bank Holiday Monday to follow. Homage to the king? Not so much, if at all. They were also cognisant that no other surviving European monarchy bothers with such an extravaganza.

No Country for the Young

For so many, the movie version of their lives as the Carolean Age commences could easily be No Country for Young Men (or women or young people of gender self-identification) where there's a cost of living crisis, a Brexit disaster they didn't vote for, and dwindling prospects of being able to buy their own homes until they are nearing fifty, if ever. The fact that pomp and pageantry is just about the only thing at which Britain tops the world league table in the food bank age offers scant consolation.

Significant, too, that polls showed a majority of the public thought, in these straitened times, the royal family and not the taxpayer ought to foot the coronation cost, a viewpoint again sounded most loudly among the young.

For different reasons, Prince Harry's attendance at his father's coronation fascinated both young sympathisers and certain strident British newspapers who pronounced his fleeting presence an unwanted, unwelcome, and a self-promoting sequel to his Netflix documentary and his Spare book savaging of his family and their courtiers.

While I'm no Sussexes' cheerleader (the hypocrisy over private jets and climate change, privacy versus publicity, is undeniable), the embittered prince does have some genuine grievances. Without doubt there were those in or around 'The Firm' for whom a pushy, opinionated mixed-race American actress wasn't their cup of tea. And, yes, some UK newspapers did stray into racist territory. What was depicting Meghan as 'Straight Outta Compton' in a Daily Mail 2 November 2016 headline if it wasn't racist as well as socially and geographically inaccurate?

Playing the tabloid game

That said, Harry is less eager to acknowledge that his mother was herself an adept player of the tabloid game. As a senior executive and editor during the 'War of the Waleses' era, I was the 'beneficiary' of briefings by sources appointed by both protagonists. And on two occasions, I heard from Diana herself, once to counter a story we'd carried from 'Team Charles', the other to alert me to a rendezvous she was having with a married man she'd become infatuated with.

The Guardian's acerbic and razor-sharp columnist Marina Hyde summed up Coronation Mania back on 18 April when she asked: 'How confidence-inspiring is any event that has thus far been defined by about 4,000 articles (and counting) about the attendance or non-attendance of a couple of guests? For a couple we keep hearing are no longer important, the Sussexes do still seem to be the only subject in town'.

Symphony of sycophancy

The tsunami of newspaper, TV, and radio coverage even had some of my monarchist friends and family complaining of overkill and crying 'enough is enough'. The particularly schmaltzy Mills & Boonesque documentary Queen Camilla: For the love of Charles (Sky May 2023) triggered memories of Private Eye's famous catchphrase 'Pass the sickbag, Alice'. At times the media was performing a symphony of sycophancy. It didn't surprise me when UK live viewing figures for the coronation turned out to be around 9 million down on those for the Queen's funeral.

Personally, the documentary flashback footage that struck me most was that of Harry, the little boy lost cruelly compelled to march behind his mother's coffin for the benefit of the world's cameras and to repair the royals' battered PR image. Those more screeching columnists portraying Meghan as the La La Land bitch who stole our chopper-flying hero prince away might pause to consider, for all her faults, she is the strong lover/mother figure Harry needs.

But pre- and post-coronation, the Duke of Sussex represents the potential spectre at the royal feast. In the days before the coronation came the opening skirmish in the first of a series of legal actions against his trio of prime newspaper targets, Rupert Murdoch's UK titles, the Mirror group, and Associated Newspapers' Daily Mail and Mail on Sunday, with allegations not just of phone hacking but of landline bugging, medical record blagging, property break-ins, and bugs planted in homes and cars.

The first big High Court trial test of Harry's claims kicked off just four days after the coronation with his headline-grabbing broadcast bulletin dominating action against the Mirror Group, with Piers Morgan's name to the fore. Never publicity averse, the former Daily

Mirror editor turned celeb TV presenter launched a pre-emptive counter strike by giving an explosive interview to the BBC's Amol Rajan that was as much a Trumpesque assault on Prince Harry's character as a simple denial of the hacking accusation being levelled at him.

Harry also cited an alleged secret pact in which his older brother received a 'huge settlement (believed to top £1m) from Murdoch's UK empire in return for a mutually beneficial deal in which the royals were to stay schtum until all the phone hackings against the newspaper group were settled (pay-outs and costs bill to date £1bn plus) and in return the Sun eased back on negative stories about Charles and Camilla. While newspaper chiefs publicly rejected the 'favourable stories' pact, it's significant that neither they nor the Palace has denied Harry's settlement assertion.

The trouble with Harry plays on

Word has it that such is Harry's self-styled 'crusade' against the British tabloids (others would describe it more a morbid obsession) that if the High Court reject him he's prepared to take his fight to the Appeal Court, the Supreme Court, and even the European courts, all in a blaze of attendant publicity. So King Charles and Prince William may have to gird their loins for a protracted, headline-grabbing international soap opera unlikely to end any time soon.

Not for nothing were Palace officials at pains to brief the media that the King raised a post-ceremony birthday toast to Prince Harry's son Archie even as his father skedaddled back to California.

Another soap opera twist looms with the legal action launched by the Trump-linked conservative US think tank The Heritage Foundation seeking to establish if Prince Harry disclosed the illegal drug-taking he admitted to in Spare as legally required in his US visa application. If not, he could potentially face expulsion. Whispers suggest the move was 'encouraged' by a couple of anti-Harry British newspapers and right-wing MPs.

Biscuits and bling for a King

Invoking the further ire of my young research sampling was when I took them through the Guardian's exhaustive investigation series into the scale of King Charles' and the royal family's wealth. Even as a media commentator and former national newspaper editor with a keen interest in the royal family, I found the figures eye-popping.

According to the Guardian the 'Biscuits and Bling' breakdown of Charles' wealth adds up to £1.82bn, with a list that includes private property (330m), Duchy of Lancaster (£653m), investments (£142m), jewellery (£533m) horses (£27m), stamp collections (£100m), cars (£6m), and art collections (£24m). While for the year ending 31 March 2022 Charles not only earned £21m personally from the Duchy but deducted millions in expenses for himself and Camilla. The Duchy, incidentally, pays no corporation tax even though it is run on corporate lines with an executive board and staff of around 150.

Many of my climate change activist young contacts were unaware of the monarchy's archaic ownership rights of most of the UK's seabed. In January the Crown Estate licensed six new offshore wind farms in a £1bn a year deal. It didn't get the tabloid coverage it merited, and although King Charles has suggested the profits will 'go to the public good, not myself', there are so far no details how.

In the 26 April edition of The New European, artfully headlined 'ACCESSION: The Coming Trials of King Charles', the respected biographer of The Queen, Clive Irving, recounted the then Prince of Wales' hostility to close scrutiny of his personal wealth. The future king stressed rather haughtily, 'I think it is of absolute importance that the monarch should have a degree of financial independence from the state […] I am not prepared to take on the position of sovereign on any other basis'.

Accession of a plutocrat?

Hardly a rallying call for the disillusioned generation. Irving argued, 'Instinctively, Charles is a plutocrat, and he lives in a plutocrat's bubble. The Queen, though very rich, was not. Consequently, Charles' version of a monarchy is beginning to look more and more like a plutocracy'.

It is undeniable that the King's wealth is soaring massively in sharp contrast to that of his ordinary subjects whose disposable income has barely risen in the last 15 years. Over the same period the taxpayer-funded Sovereign Grant has grown from £30m to £86.3m per annum. Significant, too, how my youthful sample said that a sense of respect for The Queen meant they had been far more interested in her Platinum Jubilee than King Charles' coronation or the monarchy's future. For them, a sense of resentment over Charles' wealth and privilege is destined to shape the future in the wake of 6 May's pomp and pageantry.

Some polls also revealed how many people resented Camilla being crowned Queen, with Princess Diana's ghost far from exorcised.

Surprising how many recalled that excruciating Charles/Camilla 'Tampongate' tape. Even the monarchist Daily Mail felt obliged to run a mix of sympathetic and less sympathetic articles about Camilla after one reader survey reflected only 13 per cent welcomed her becoming Queen.

Can soft power save the monarchy?

For many of Charles's media supporters, 'soft power' is the buzz term. The respected author of two acclaimed Charles' biographies, Catherine Mayer, who was granted remarkable access to his inner circle, told me at the 15 March 2023 Society of Editors conference, 'The King and Prince William are well aware of the importance of soft power. The threat to the monarchy is not revolution but the danger of the evolution of irrelevance, apathy, boredom, particularly among the young, together with the potential for both the mainstream media and social media becoming seriously disenchanted. That's the challenge facing both the King and the Prince of Wales and soft power is a way to combat that'.

Paradoxically, perhaps, another poll in the i newspaper on 8 May provided King Charles with food for thought when it showed young people in particular warming to the notion of a more 'political monarch' who spoke his mind and intervened on the 'big issues'. By curious coincidence the next day's Daily Mail went off adulatory piste to splash on a claim that, not long before becoming monarch, Charles and then prime minister Boris Johnson 'squared up' to each other over the then Prince calling the government's Rwanda policy over migrants 'appalling', with the PM accusing him of political meddling. It was based on a claim by former No 10 Communications Director Guto Harris, the former BBC journalist who also served as Johnson's communications guru when he was London Mayor.

For Charles, William, and even Prince George the monarchical clock ticks ever louder and the juggling act needed to somehow keep the public and media onside ever trickier: Game of Thrones indeed.

About the contributor

Paul Connew is a media commentator, broadcaster, ex-editor of the Sunday Mirror, deputy editor of the Daily Mirror, former Mirror group US bureau chief and (pre-phone hacking) deputy editor of the News of the World. He writes and broadcasts on the media and politics for a number of organisations including the BBC, Sky News, CNN, GB News, LBC,

Australian Broadcasting, Al-Jazeera, The New European, and The Drum website. A regular judge of the British Press Awards, he has been a contributing author for a dozen previous hackademic books. He also works with Netflix and Amazon on documentary projects.

Chapter 23

Irish republicanism and the monarchy

In succeeding his mother, Queen Elizabeth II, her eldest son became Charles III 'by the Grace of God of the United Kingdom of Great Britain and Northern Ireland and of His other Realms and Territories King, Head of the Commonwealth, Defender of the Faith'. As the King is aware, the role he formally accepted at his 6 May coronation is somewhat different to that when his mother became queen at her 1953 coronation. **Steven McCabe** reflects on the relationship between the monarchy, the media, and Irish republicanism

King Charles III is expected to more explicitly demonstrate sensitivity to the challenge of being supreme ruler of every citizen of the United Kingdom, regardless of their beliefs. Charles' kingdom appears increasingly disunited, none more so than in the part in which tension and hostility still exists between the two major communities, Northern Ireland. Although conflict ended there as a result of the 1997 Good Friday Agreement, it has left lingering distrust and mutual suspicion. The UK's departure from the European Union has heightened unease and undermined peace. King Charles is only too well aware of the personal loss of 'the troubles' when, in August 1979, his 'Honorary Grandfather', great uncle Lord Louis Mountbatten was murdered by the Provisional IRA (Irish Republican Army).

King Charles will also be fully cognisant of the fact that as Commander-in-Chief of British armed forces he's considered by the Nationalist/Republican community in Northern Ireland to carry ultimate responsibility for both current and past transgressions by crown forces. As King Charles will surely be aware, 'the troubles', resulting in over 3,500 deaths (military personnel and civilians) and well over 47,500 injured, some terribly, is viewed by Irish Republicans as the culmination of centuries of frequently cruel intervention, commenced in the sixteenth century by King Henry VIII. Charles, who formally became King at his coronation on 6 May, will be assumed to publicly continue the acts of reconciliation acknowledging the hurt and brutality carried out by military personnel begun under his mother. The new King will know that engaging in such acts requires cooperation from the media which has not been unbiased and impartial in their reporting.

Partition and 'the troubles'

Tudor conquest commenced under Henry VIII and resulted in Ireland's citizens becoming unwilling witnesses of or active participants in proxy wars and rebellions. The latter exacted brutal retribution by crown forces, an expression used by Irish republicans regularly during 'the troubles' (Hawes-Bilger, 2007). One policy, plantation, involving encouragement of large numbers of English and Scottish Protestants to settle in Ireland through sequestration of land owned by Catholics, particularly in Ulster, increased resentment. Uprisings were harshly suppressed. Eventually, in the late nineteenth century, recognition of the difficulties of maintaining rule over Ireland led to a campaign for home rule by the Liberal Party. This created a crisis and was not universally welcomed by the press (Parry, 1989). Many commentators saw it as surrender of the King's authority and akin to abandonment of protestants loyal to the crown.

Anger by Irish Republicans eventually resulted in full-scale rebellion, the Easter Uprising in April 1916. Though this was to lead to the eventual creation in 1922 of the Irish Republic and the separate state of Northern Ireland, the act of rebellion during war with Germany was widely reported in the press as sedition and organised by treacherous zealots disloyal to King George (The British Newspaper Archive, 2023). Government restriction of the Irish media in reporting events surrounding the rebellion during wartime was resented within Ireland (Kenneally, 2023). Such restriction was to be a characteristic of the British government during conflict in Northern Ireland between 1969 and 1997.

However, many press outlets reported events in a way partial to the army and security personnel loyally defending the Queen's writ against bloodthirsty murderers (Henderson and Little, 2018; Henderson and Little, 2022). Words such as 'savages' and 'psychopaths' regularly appeared to describe those engaged in violence. Those giving their support were considered no better. Campaigning Derry-based journalist Eamonn McCann, who witnessed Bloody Sunday, wrote, 'Most British people have a distorted view of what is happening in Northern Ireland. This is because they believe what they read' (McCann, 1972). Further on, McCann contends that reporters writing copy critical of 'the establishment and its representatives' found it to be rejected or heavily edited. As he concludes, 'The news from Northern Ireland has been a compound lie'. The clear message largely presented by the media was clear: so-called 'physical force' republicanism and those giving them succour were enemies of the monarch and all who supported freedom under Queen Elizabeth II.

'Oliver's Army': Cromwell and Elvis (Costello)

'Oliver's Army' is a 1979 pop song by Elvis Costello. Eminently danceable, it's unlikely most hearing it were aware it's based on Costello, who is second-generation Irish, witnessing harassment of young men and women (presumably Catholic) whilst performing in Belfast. Its title refers to Oliver Cromwell, known for unbridled brutality visited on opponents. Inevitably, the Irish would suffer similar (and worse). Sackings by Cromwell's troops of Wexford and Drogheda resulted in thousands of innocent civilians being killed. Cromwell wrote subsequently, 'I am persuaded that this is a righteous judgment of God upon these barbarous wretches'.

When internment was introduced in Northern Ireland in August 1971 and during which innocent men were detained, and tensions among the Catholic community heightened, Paddy McGuigan's song, 'The Men Behind the Wire', included the lines:

> Not for them a judge or jury
> Or indeed a crime at all
> Being Irish means they're guilty
> So we're guilty one and all [...]
> Cromwell's men are here again
> England's name again is sullied
> In the eyes of honest men.

Within the Nationalist/Republican community, apart from partisan propaganda outlets such as An Phoblacht, the newspaper published by Sinn Féin, the political wing of the Provisional IRA, media reporting of events they were experiencing presented events in a way frequently at odds with reality.

1979: crunch year

Though there'd been violent years earlier in the decade, 1979 was to prove traumatic for many. 'Securitisation', effectively treating certain areas of Northern Ireland as war zones, introduced under Labour's Roy Mason, would become even more pronounced under new Prime Minister Margaret Thatcher. She explicitly viewed all who engaged in violence in pursuits of political goals as criminals. The press generally supported this stance. Any reporter or media outlet presenting alternative perspectives could anticipate unsympathetic treatment, as McCann had pointed out in 1972, through censorship and threat of legal action (McCabe, 2020).

After the murder of Lord Mountbatten, the royal family were in no doubt that they were viewed by some, though not all, Irish Republicans, as 'legitimate targets'. The murder of a member of the royal family, as well as others killed in the explosion on his boat whilst sailing off the coast of Sligo, as well as the fact that 17 soldiers were killed the same day in a double bombing in Warrenpoint in County Down, produced inevitable reaction in the press. Calls for the return of capital punishment, internment, and greater security measures to be used against Irish Republicans merely created a climate in which increased antagonism fed further resentment of the role of the state and, by virtue, its head, the monarch. Some commentators reporting on events in Northern Ireland, weary of the apparently ceaseless cycles of violence, revenge attacks, and imposition of increased security, primarily on those living in Nationalist/Republican areas, appeared to believe the conflict was endless.

Peace comes; the Queen responds

An end to conflict, which came in 1997, is well documented and based on mutual respect by all protagonists (McCabe, 2019). Though politicians were essential to achieving peace, it became apparent that a central element of rapprochement, intended as part of reconciliation, was that the monarch, Queen Elizabeth II, should engage in symbolic acts of reaching out. This came in various forms. In 2011, as part of a royal visit to Ireland, she laid a wreath at Dublin's Garden of Remembrance to commemorate fallen Irish republicans. The following year in June whilst on a visit to Belfast she shook hands with former Provisional IRA deputy commander Martin McGuinness at Belfast's Lyric Theatre. With the assistance of the media, a clear message was being sent. Queen Elizabeth was prepared to consign centuries-old enmity to history in the quest for peace for all citizens.

King Charles continues reconciliation?

Conscious of the need to underline his credentials as King to all citizens, shortly after his mother's death, Charles III visited Northern Ireland to meet people mourning the loss of Queen Elizabeth. As part of this visit, he met with the vice president of Sinn Féin and (putative) First Minister, Michelle O'Neill, at Hillsborough Castle. With huge symbolism, and not without controversy, O'Neill received an invitation to King Charles III's coronation on 6 May which she accepted.

This bodes well for the future and will undoubtedly improve Charles' standing among Catholics in Northern Ireland. However, he will be acutely aware that in a post-Brexit era, gaining the support of one community should not be at the expense of those who have traditionally been loyal to the monarch as demonstrated on the many murals which exist. Though Charles III surely recognises that being a monarch who is as universally respected and admired as his mother by all communities in Northern Ireland is no easy matter, he's made a decent start.

References

Cordula Hawes-Bilger (2007) War Zone Language : Linguistic Aspects of the Conflict in Northern Ireland, Tübingen: Narr Francke Attempto Verlag.
Deric Henderson and Ivan Little (2018) Reporting the Troubles: Journalists Tell Their Stories of the Northern Ireland Conflict, Newtownards: Blackstaff Press.
Deric Henderson and Ivan Little (2022), Reporting the Troubles 2: More Journalists Tell Their Stories of the Northern Ireland Conflict, Newtownards: Blackstaff Press.
Ian Kenneally (2023), 'The Role of the Press in 1916', The Irish Revolution Project Website, University College Cork, https://www.ucc.ie/en/theirishrevolution/collections/the-story-of-1916/chapter-5-the-aftermath-of-the-1916-rising/the-role-of-the-press-in-1916/, accessed 28 April
Steven McCabe (2019) 'Northern Ireland, conflict and 'otherness' and the evolution of the Good Friday Agreement', in John Mair, Steven McCabe, Neil Fowler, and Leslie Budd (eds) Brexit and Northern Ireland – Bordering On Confusion, Goring: Bite-Sized Books.
Steven McCabe (2020), 'Shot by both sides — an examination of the

challenges faced by the BBC during 'the Troubles'', in John Mair (ed) The BBC — A Winter of Discontent?, Goring: Bite-Sized Books.
Eamonn McCann (1972) The British Press and Northern Ireland, Northern Ireland: Northern Ireland Socialist Research Centre.
Ann Parry (1989), 'The Home Rule Crisis and the 'Liberal' Periodicals 1886-1895: Three Case Studies', Victorian Periodicals Review, Vol. 22, No. 1 (Spring), pp 18-30
The British Newspaper Archive (2023), 'The Easter Rising: As documented in the British newspapers, 1916', The British Newspaper Archive Website, https://blog.britishnewspaperarchive.co.uk/2016/03/22/the-easter-rising-as-documented-in-the-british-newspapers-1916/, accessed 29 April

About the contributor

Dr Steve McCabe is Associate Professor at Birmingham City University where he's been an academic since 1987. He is a political economist, and has published widely, including on Northern Ireland. He writes and comments regularly in the national and international media on politics and the economy. Recent books edited by him include Brexit and Northern Ireland – Bordering on Confusion, English Regions After Brexit: Examining Potential Change through Devolved Power, Exploring the Green Economy: Issues, Challenges and Benefits, Green Manufacturing: What this Involves and How to Achieve Success, Stop House Prices Rising!, and Another Way: A Call for a New Direction in British Foreign Policy and Defence Policy?

Chapter 24

The Queen is dead; republic now!

The 8 September 2022 death of Queen Elizabeth II prompted sympathetic responses from some most unlikely quarters. **Phil Butland**, *of theleftberlin.com, considers what this told us about the British monarchy, public figures, and national and international reaction to that event*

On 8 September 2022 a 96-year-old woman died. Nothing unusual there. On average, 1,679 people die in the UK every day. But this time round, everyone from the British Kebab Awards to The Prodigy made gushingly sycophantic statements. Britain's idiot prime minister-in-waiting Liz Truss, called the deceased 'among the world's greatest-ever leaders'.

As Britain was sent into ten days of enforced commemoration, the madness also spread to Germany. Chancellor Olaf Scholz called her a 'role model and inspiration for millions', while Berlin mayor Franziska Giffey said that the 'power of her great personality has always fascinated us Berliners'. Brandenburger Tor was lit up in the colours of the Union Flag in her honour.

Even John Lydon, who as Johnny Rotten once sang, 'God save the queen / She ain't no human being / There is no future / In England's dreaming', got involved. He posted the following message on social media: 'Rest in peace Queen Elizabeth II. Send her victorious From all at johnlydon.com'.

Extinction Rebellion had been planning a so-called Festival of Resistance in London. They issued a statement, saying 'Due to today's news about the passing of Queen Elizabeth, the Rebellion Planning team, and other groups involved, have made the difficult decision to postpone the Festival of Resistance this weekend in London until further notice'. So, there is no time to waste in resisting climate change — unless a privileged old woman dies.

The Trades Union Conference (TUC) postponed its conference. The post and rail unions called off planned strikes, although, interestingly, barristers will continue to strike. Leader of the RMT rail union Mick Lynch said, 'RMT joins the whole nation in paying its respects to Queen Elizabeth'.

This is the same Mick Lynch who a few days before proudly declared his love of James Connolly. In a television appearance, he asked his interviewer: "Do you know who James Connolly is? He was an Irish socialist republican and he educated himself and started non-sectarian trade unionism in Ireland. And he was a hero of the Irish revolution."

James Connolly was indeed an Irish revolutionary who wrote the following: 'A people mentally poisoned by the adulation of royalty can never attain to that spirit of self-reliant democracy necessary for the attainment of social freedom'. Unfortunately Connolly's most famous supporter is showing exactly this sort of adulation.

Just like us?

Labour leader Keir Starmer tweeted, 'Above the clashes of politics, she stood not for what the nation fought over, but what it agreed upon'. But just how much did the life of this privately educated woman with 30 castles resemble that of a normal pensioner?

One of the last acts of Elizabeth Windsor was to pay £12 million to cover the court fees of her son Andrew. Andrew is accused of sexually abusing Virginia Giuffre when she was a teenager, and the evidence against him looks compelling. It is not even a matter of dispute that he regularly partied with known paedophiles and sex traffickers.

Andrew is not the first sexual predator to visit royal palaces. Serial rapist Jimmy Savile used palace visits to seize young women and lick their arms. When Prince Charles and Princess Diana had marital difficulties, they employed Savile as a counsellor. Charles asked him to help improve the image of his brother's soon to be ex-wife Sarah Ferguson.

How much?

While many British pensioners die of hypothermia each winter, the royals have an annual gas bill of £2.5 million. This is not something they find difficult to pay. Forbes magazine estimated last year that the Royal Family is worth $28 billion. In 2022 the Sovereign Grant, which replaced the Civil List, allocated them £86.3 million, compared with

£42.8 five years previously. This money is paid by the British taxpayer.

As Bailey Schulz reported in USA Today, the Queen's 'personal assets from investments, real estate, jewels and more have an estimated worth of $500 million'. Prince Charles's Duchy of Cornwall inherits all the wealth of people who die in Cornwall without making a will. His estate, worth £1billion, now passes to Prince William.

The royal family own 1.4 percent of all land in England, including nearly all of Regent Street and most of the UK seabed. They have their own train costing at least £800,000 a year, and a helicopter costing nearly £1 million. A new royal yacht is being built costing £250 million. Even Elizabeth II's funeral will cost British taxpayers £6 billion.

Ten million pounds of the Queen's private money was invested in offshore tax havens like the Cayman Islands and Bermuda. It is a step forward that she at least feels the need to hide her tax. She only agreed to pay any income tax at all in 1992, when the popularity of the royals was at rock bottom.

During the Covid-19 pandemic, the Queen gained an exemption from the ongoing eviction ban and evicted a couple from one of her many properties. The reason? Using a communal plug socket to charge their electric car. In 2004 the Queen asked a state poverty fund used to help low-income families to pay for heating Buckingham Palace.

Notwithstanding their vast wealth, the royals were not prepared to look after their own family. In 1941 Nerissa and Katherine Bowes-Lyon, Elizabeth's first cousins, were sent to the 'Royal Earlswood Asylum for Mental Defectives'. They each had a mental age of around three and never learned to talk.

In 1961 they were recorded as deceased although Nerissa actually died in 1986 and was buried in a pauper's grave. Katherine died in 2014. There is no record of anyone visiting them. A nurse reported: "They never received anything at Christmas either, not a sausage." The royals sent the hospital £125 a year for their care, but never publicly acknowledged their existence.

The legacy of colonialism

The British monarchy has always had a close relationship with colonialism and imperialism. Elizabeth's great-great-grandmother Victoria styled herself the Empress of India and presided over the expansion of the British empire.

When Princess Elizabeth learned she was going to be queen she was representing Britain's colonial interests in Kenya. Later that year,

British troops brutally suppressed the Mau Mau rebellion in the same country. The New York Times reported, 'The clampdown on Kenyans, which began just months after the queen ascended the throne, led to the establishment of a vast system of detention camps and the torture, rape, castration and killing of tens of thousands of people'.

The monarch is the head of the British army, and has the right to recruit, appoint commissioned officers, and negotiate the stationing of British troops on foreign soil. Under Elizabeth's watch, British troops invaded Egypt after President Nasser nationalised the Suez Canal, shot dead 14 unarmed civilians in Derry, and acted as bag carriers on countless US imperial adventures.

The royal family continues to benefit from the plunder of the colonial years. The new queen Camilla will inherit the crown which contains the Koh-i-Noor diamond, valued at $400 million but considered to be priceless. Indian economist Utsa Patnaik estimates that goods stolen between 1765 and 1938 by the British from the Indian subcontinent alone were worth $45 trillion.

The royal family continues to aid imperialism. When BAE systems sold 72 Typhoon fighter jets to the Saudi Arabian dictatorship, Prince Charles was in Riyadh dancing with Saudi princes on the evening before the deal was signed. According to Andrew Smith from the Campaign Against the Arms Trade: "It is clear that Prince Charles has been used by the UK government and BAE Systems as an arms dealer".

In 1974 a majority of Australians had the temerity to vote for the Labour politician Gough Whitlam. But the following year it was the Queen's representative who sacked Whitlam and ushered in a Conservative government. So much for the royals being above politics.

Racism

Elizabeth's husband Philip was famed for his racist remarks. The British media quaintly reported this as 'gaffes'. On a state visit to China in 1986 he told British students that if they stayed in the country they would go 'slitty eyed'. In 1998 he asked a British student in Papua New Guinea, "You managed not to get eaten, then?". Four years later, in Australia, he asked an Aboriginal man, "Still throwing spears?" Philip's brother-in-law was a close aide of SS chief Heinrich Himmler.

Philip was not the only racist in the family. Elizabeth's mother was fond of calling black people 'nig-nogs'. When Stephen Fry told the Queen's sister Margaret that he was Jewish, she 'expressed her horror by shouting to everybody else at her table, "He's a Jew. He's a Jew".

Margaret once told the Mayor of Chicago that 'the Irish are pigs, all pigs'.

We are often told the 'tragic story' of Elizabeth's uncle Edward who had to abdicate because he wanted to marry a divorcee. The truth is that the establishment were more worried that both Edward and his fiancée were open Nazis who regularly visited Hitler in the run-up to the Second World War. In 2015 The Sun released exclusive photos of Edward teaching a young Princess Elizabeth and her sister to make a Nazi salute under the headline 'Their Royal Heilnesses'.

Until at least the 1960s Buckingham Palace banned 'coloured immigrants or foreigners' from work. Even now the monarch is exempt from several laws, including those concerning racial, ethnic, or sexual equality.

The racism continues to the present. When Meghan Markle was expecting the Queen's grandson, members of the British royal family expressed 'concerns and conversations' about how dark her son's skin would be. Her husband Harry said that racism was a 'large part' of the motivation for the couple leaving the UK.

Do we need a figurehead?

Shortly after Elizabeth's death the Blairite journalist Polly Toynbee wrote an egregious piece in The Guardian in which she stated, 'Every nation needs a figurehead; and, however perverse the sheer randomness of being born into that role, she did it with remarkable skill and dignity'. In other words, know your place, plebs.

But do British people really need a figurehead to unite behind? Working class Britons have more in common with other working class people in Berlin and Kolkata than with a Tory government that claims that we're all in this together while attacking living standards and handing over the profits to their friends in the City. We don't need a fake unity with the people responsible for keeping our wages low and our rents high.

We are asked to lay off the queen because she was an old woman, just a symbol. But what she symbolises is exactly the problem: empire, colonialism, and the fact that if you're born into the right family, you're guaranteed a well-paying job.

The monarchy cannot survive without the racist belief in birth privilege. As John Mullen has argued, 'The existence of a king or queen represents the principle that one family is born superior to another — more deserving of privilege, purer, more virtuous, because of their bloodline. This is the idea that plagued humanity from ancient slavery to Nazis'.

It is not just that royals get their jobs because of birth rather than merit. It is much worse than that. They are all born into privilege, privately educated, and do not understand how most of us live. It is not a coincidence that so many of them end up as far right racists. Even the progressive one who married a black woman went to a fancy dress party in a Nazi uniform 'for a laugh'.

The royals are not representative of the country as a whole. They are representatives of their class. When Paris Hilton tweeted that the Queen was the 'original girl boss', she was right, even though she didn't understand the implications of what she was saying.

People say that the monarchy is above politics, that the role is purely symbolic. If this is true, why must the British people pay them so much? Why are Elizabeth's relatives allowed to keep the expensive booty of colonial expropriation? When the victims of colonialism rightly claim the reparations they are owed, their first stop after the British Museum should be Buckingham Palace.

What happens now?

So what happens now that Britain is being ruled by a man who is much less popular than his mother, employs someone to iron his shoelaces and once fantasised about being his mistress's tampon?

There's a shift going on in British society which we shouldn't overstate but isn't insignificant. A Statista poll in 2022 found that 'younger age groups are progressively more likely to oppose the monarchy, with 31 percent of 18-24 year olds opting instead for an elected head of state'. This was under the relatively popular Elizabeth. Another poll in 2022 showed that two-thirds of Britons did not want Charles to succeed his mother.

The British royals have been declining in support for several decades. This is why my friend Jacinta Nandi is trying to popularise the hashtag #THETIMEISNOW. Although I think that the time was 1,000 years ago, rising prices and a growing discrepancy between poor and rich means that Britons can no longer afford the royals. It's time for them to go.

About the contributor

Phil Butland was born in England but now lives in Germany, where he serves on the editorial board of theleftberlin.com.

Afterword

From consensus to contention: Changing public attitudes towards the monarchy

The British monarchy is still a relatively popular institution. However, it no longer enjoys the near universal consensus of support that it once enjoyed. **Sir John Curtice** finds that King Charles III and his heirs will need to find a strategy that enhances the monarchy's reputation in the eyes of the British public

Asking questions on polls about the monarchy once seemed a waste of time. Its role and status were little questioned. This picture was confirmed by the results of one of the earliest polls that did address the subject. Shortly after the 21 June 1969 airing of a widely watched BBC television documentary, Royal Family, NOP found that 88 per cent believed the monarchy was 'good for Britain'. That message was echoed by the first British Social Attitudes survey in 1983, which asked, 'How important or unimportant do you think it is for Britain to continue to have a monarchy?'. As many as 65 per cent said it was 'very important' and another 21 per cent that it was 'quite important' — a combined total of 86 per cent. Equally, when in 1984 Ipsos asked whether, on balance, 'Britain would be better off or worse off if the monarchy was abolished or do you think it would make no difference?', as many as 77 per cent reckoned the country would be worse off.

Cracks

But these proved to be high water marks. During the 1980s more than one royal marriage began to hit the rocks, cutting across the image of a model family that had been portrayed in the 1969 BBC documentary. At the same time, the monarchy's finances and privileged tax status became the subject of increasing scrutiny and criticism. As a result, even before what the late Queen herself termed her 'annus horribilis', that is, 1992 when the marriages of three of her children came to an end and Windsor Castle suffered a devastating fire, public attitudes had already become markedly more critical. According to Ipsos, the proportion who thought that Britain would be worse off without the monarchy, already down by the beginning of 1991 to little more than a half (56 per cent), plummeted by the end of 1992 to just 37 per cent.

It soon became clear that the crown was now a little more contentious. When in 1994 the British Social Attitudes survey repeated its 1983 question, the proportion who thought it was 'very' important to have a monarchy had fallen to 31 per cent, while those saying it was 'very' or 'quite' important was down to 65 per cent. Meanwhile, although three polls conducted by Ipsos in 1993 and 1994 found on average that as many as 71 per cent would favour Britain becoming a monarchy, there was now a discernible minority of 18 per cent who wanted a republic.

Stability

Still, this picture changed little over the subsequent twenty years. In eleven readings taken between 1995 and 2008, on average 31 per cent told BSA it was 'very important' to have a monarchy, while 65 per cent said it was 'very' or 'quite important'. Similarly, in 18 polls it conducted between 1997 and 2006, on average Ipsos found that 72 per cent wanted to keep the monarchy, while 18 per cent stated that Britain should become a republic. Although lower than it once was, public support for the institution had at least seemed to have plateaued at what was still a relatively high level.

In 2011 and 2012 the Queen made much lauded trips to Northern Ireland and the Irish Republic, symbolically healing divisions on both sides of the border most notably by shaking of the hand of the former IRA commander, Martin McGuinness. This particularly striking display of the monarchy's 'soft power' appeared to be appreciated. In both years, three-quarters (75 per cent) told BSA it was important to have a monarchy. Equally, in three polls conducted in 2012, also the year of the Queen's Diamond Jubilee, on average 79 per cent advised Ipsos that they preferred a monarchy, while support for a republic slipped to 15 per cent.

That improvement was not, however, sustained. By 2018 BSA was reporting that the percentage saying it was important to have a monarchy was back down to 68 per cent. Meanwhile, whereas YouGov (in response to a question it first asked the previous year) found in July

2012 that 75 per cent thought that Britain should continue to be a monarchy and only 15 per cent preferred 'an elected head of state', by 2018 the proportion backing a monarchy was down to 66 per cent, although support for an elected head of state was still no more than 18 per cent.

Contention

Meanwhile, during the final years of Queen Elizabeth's reign, cracks appeared once more in the image of a stable 'Royal Family'. In 2019, Prince Andrew was forced to withdraw from public life following a disastrous television interview in respect of allegations of improper sexual behaviour and a subsequent out-of-court settlement with the complainant. In early 2020, King Charles' younger son, Harry, and his wife, Meghan, opted to pursue a private life in the US following a well-publicised and still continuing falling out with other members of the family.

Support for the monarchy fell yet further. In the 2021 British Social Attitudes survey a record low of 55 per cent said it was important to have a monarchy. Equally, an Ipsos poll in November 2021 found that those preferring a monarchy had dropped to a new low of 60 per cent, while 21 per cent supported a republic. At the same time, the proportion who thought that Britain would be better off without a monarchy was, at 39 per cent, back down to a level similar to that recorded in 1992. Meanwhile, YouGov were reporting in March 2022 that just 59 per cent now backed a continuation of the monarchy, while 24 per cent would prefer an elected head of state. Indeed, the same company also reported in May 2022 that just 56 per cent thought the monarchy was 'good for Britain', a far cry from the 88 per cent figure reported by NOP in 1969. Despite her personal popularity, the late Queen Elizabeth bequeathed to her son an institution that, while still backed by a majority, had become markedly less popular during her reign.

The death of the late Queen and the subsequent period of national mourning did see some short-term increase in support for the monarchy. However, more recent readings are much like those taken shortly before her death. In January 2023 a National Centre for Social Research survey that re-interviewed people who had previously been questioned for British Social Attitudes again found that only 55 per cent believed it was important to have a monarchy. Two polls undertaken by Ipsos in January and March on average found 65 per cent in favour of a monarchy and a record high of 24 per cent supporting a republic. The same company also reported that the proportion who thought that Britain would be worse off without the monarchy was still, at most, around 40 per cent. Meanwhile on average in four polls conducted by YouGov in March and April, shortly before coronation of King Charles III, 60 per cent said they preferred a monarchy, while 25 per cent wanted an elected head of state.

Other companies that polled in the weeks before the coronation recorded similar figures, albeit in response to slightly different questions. Between them, the polls that were undertaken during in March and April 2023 suggested that a little under three in five now support the monarchy, while one in four would prefer an alternative. While the crown is still popular, its merits and demerits have now become the subject of media commentary and public debate.

Division

The monarchy is not just less popular than it once was — it is also decidedly short of support among some sections of British society. Younger people have always been less keen on the monarchy than older people, but have then come to value the institution as they have got older. However, today's younger generation are particularly less likely to be enamoured of the monarchy. For example, according to the latest National Centre survey (January 2023), only 12 per cent of those aged under 35 think it is 'very important' to have a monarchy, 30 points below the equivalent figure for those aged 55 and over. In contrast, as recently as 2015 as many as 32 per cent of those aged under 35 expressed that view, only 16 points adrift of the figure for those 55 or more. There is a risk that today's youngest generation might never be as supportive of the monarchy as their predecessors.

The greater racial diversity of British society presents a challenge too. A survey of those from a minority ethnic background conducted by YouGov in April 2023 found a near even split between those who would prefer a monarchy (38 per cent) and those who would like an elected head of state (39 per cent). The crown is also less popular in Scotland and Northern Ireland. Two polls conducted by YouGov and Lord Ashcroft in Scotland in the run-up to King Charles' coronation both found only 46 per cent preferring a monarchy to a republic, ten to twelve points adrift of the figure in parallel polls of Britain as a whole. Meanwhile, Lord Ashcroft's polling suggests that those in Northern Ireland who would vote in a referendum to keep the monarchy (42 per cent) are slightly outnumbered by those who would back a republic (46 per cent). In both countries the monarchy finds itself inextricably caught up the debate about their constitutional status: the balance of opinion among supporters of independence in Scotland and nationalists in Northern Ireland is tilted heavily against the monarchy.

The future

Britain's monarchy can no longer assume it has an indefinite shelf life. The soap opera that has repeatedly surrounded the 'Royal Family' has been toxic and has done nothing to help demonstrate the value of an institution that some regard as unbelievably wealthy. Indeed, it may be time to ditch the notion of the monarchy as a model 'family' – after all, the late Queen's children now reflect the rest of British society in the complexity of their family relationships. Meanwhile, the potential opportunity to connect with Britain's minority ethnic community via Prince Harry's marriage to a woman of mixed heritage has been missed.

But all is not necessarily lost. The public appreciation of the late Queen's visits to Ireland a decade ago suggests the monarchy's future lies in wielding its 'soft power' to bring people together at home and to project Britain's image abroad — including well beyond a Commonwealth whose own ties to the monarchy may soon be few and far between (Ashcroft 2023). If the 'mystique' of the monarchy is to be preserved, it will need to be used to good effect.

References

Lord Ashcroft (2023) Uncharted Realms: The Future of the Monarchy in the UK and around the World. Available at http://lordashcroftpolls.com/wp-content/uploads/2023/05/Uncharted-Realms-Lord-Ashcroft-Polls-May-2023.pdf

About the contributor

Sir John Curtice is Professor of Politics at the University of Strathclyde and Senior Research Fellow, National Centre for Social Research, and 'The UK in a Changing Europe'. President of the British Polling Council, he has been co-editor of the annual series of British Social Attitudes reports since 1994. He is also a regular media commentator on public opinion and electoral behaviour in the UK.

Printed in Great Britain
by Amazon